CULTURES OF THE WORLD

BAHAMAS

Robert Barlas

MARSHALL CAVENDISH
New York • London • Sydney

Reference edition reprinted 2001 by
Marshall Cavendish Corporation
99 White Plains Road
Tarrytown
New York 10591

© Times Media Private Limited 2000

Originated and designed by
Times Books International, an imprint of
Times Media Private Limited, a member of the
Times Publishing Group

Printed in Malaysia

Library of Congress Cataloging-in-Publication Data:

Barlas, Robert.
    Bahamas / Robert Barlas.
        p. cm.—(Cultures of the world)
    Includes bibliographical references and index.
    Summary: Introduces the geography, history, government,
    economy, religion, language, arts, leisure activities, festivals,
    food, and people of this archipelago lying in the Atlantic
    Ocean off the coast of Florida.
    ISBN 0-7614-0992-0 (lib. bdg.)
    1. Bahamas—Juvenile literature. [1. Bahamas.] I. Title.
II. Series.

F1651.2 .B37 2000
972.96—dc21   99-088028
                    CIP
                    AC

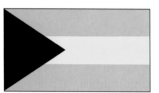

THE COMMONWEALTH OF THE BAHAMAS consists of about 700 islands and cays and nearly 2,000 tiny islands that are little more than rock formations jutting above sea level. This single country is spread out over 90,000 square miles (233,100 square km) of the Atlantic Ocean, off the southwestern coast of Florida. Most people know the Bahamas as a popular tourist destination, famous for its vast sandy beaches and opportunities to snorkel and scuba-dive.

These idyllic tropical islands have a colorful history: they have been a pirates' kingdom, part of the vast British Empire, and today an independent country with a democratically elected government. Over the centuries the Bahamas also acquired its migrant population, with the result that its people are as diverse as its history. The Bahamas is still in many ways a tropical paradise for its citizens and for tourists, but Bahamians look to a future full of potential still to be realized.

CONTENTS

Dolls on sale at the Straw Market in Nassau.

CONTENTS

A boy stretches to mail his letter at a typically British red pillar box.

GEOGRAPHY

THE BAHAMAS is an archipelago lying in the Atlantic Ocean off the coast of Florida in the United States. South of the Bahamas are Cuba, Haiti, and the Dominican Republic, while in the southeast are the Turks and Caicos Islands. The Tropic of Cancer runs through the middle of the Bahamas.

Exactly how many islands there are in the Bahamas depends on whether one counts every cay, even the ones that are no more than lumps of rock sticking out of the sea. Most references, however, agree that there are 700 significant islands and cays. As for the total number, some sources say there are 2,000, while other estimates are as high as 3,000. Such uncertainty may raise questions as to the total land area of the Bahamas, but officially it is 5,382 square miles (13,940 square km). The islands range in size from a tiny cay just a mile wide to Andros Island, the largest island in the Bahamas at 2,300 square miles (6,000 square km). The capital of the Bahamas, Nassau, is on the island of New Providence.

A great percentage of the Bahamian population lives on fewer than 20 of the major islands. The 10 most populated islands of the Bahamas, in order of population size, are New Providence, Grand Bahama, Eleuthera (including Harbour Island just offshore), the Abacos, Andros, the Exumas, Long Island, Cat Island, the Biminis, and the Inaguas.

Opposite: **Clear turquoise water surrounds the tiny island of Green Turtle Cay, off Great Abaco.**

Left: **A bird's-eye view of Grand Bahama.**

7

TOPOGRAPHY

The sea around the Bahamas is mostly shallow, although there are deep places such as the Tongue of the Ocean trench between Andros and the Exumas, which is more than a mile deep. The islands are quite low-lying, often no higher than 20 feet (6 m) and rarely exceeding 150 feet (46 m). The highest point, Mt. Alvernia on Cat Island, is only 206 feet (63 m) high.

THE BLUE HOLES The islands of the Bahamas sit on top of countless generations of sea fossils and disintegrated coral rising from the seabed. This sedimentary foundation, called oolitic limestone, is a soft rock that is easily eroded by mild acids such as rainwater. Over time, erosion has created sinkholes.

Beneath the surface of some of the major islands is a subterranean world of caves filled with a combination of fresh and sea water (sea water easily seeps through the limestone)—these are the blue holes of the Bahamas. The blue holes have been explored extensively since the 1950s,

The name "Bahamas" is derived from Baja Mar, *Spanish for "shallow sea." The word "cay" is derived from* cairi, *meaning "island," which comes from the Lucayans, the earliest inhabitants of the Bahamas. They called themselves the* lukku-cairi—*island people.*

IS THE BAHAMAS PART OF THE CARIBBEAN OR THE WEST INDIES?

Both the *Encyclopedia Britannica* and the *Random House Webster's College Dictionary* say the West Indies includes the Greater Antilles (Cuba, Dominican Republic, Haiti, Jamaica, and Puerto Rico), Lesser Antilles, and the Bahamas. The dictionary defines the Caribbean as "the islands and countries of the Caribbean Sea," the sea being bounded by Central America, the West Indies, and South America. By that definition, the Bahamas, as part of the West Indies, does not belong to the Caribbean.

Politically, however, the Bahamas is included whenever the Caribbean as a collective entity is mentioned: for example, the Bahamas belongs to an intergovernmental organization called the Caribbean Development Bank, and it is a member of the Caribbean Community and Common Market (CARICOM for short). The Bahamas is also a beneficiary of the Caribbean Basin Initiative.

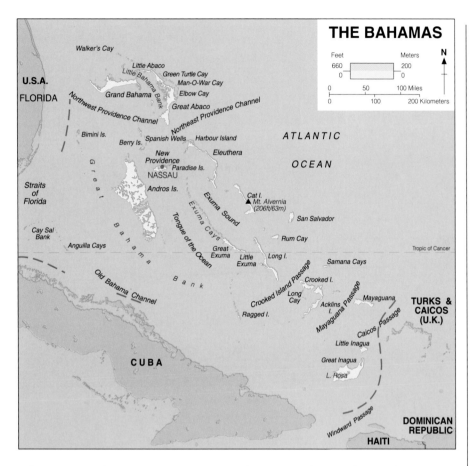

THE BAHAMAS

Feet		Meters	N
660		200	
0		0	

0	50	100 Miles
0	100	200 Kilometers

Walker's Cay

Little Abaco
Little Bahama Bank
Green Turtle Cay
Man-O-War Cay
Grand Bahama
Elbow Cay
Great Abaco

U.S.A.
FLORIDA

Northwest Providence Channel

Northeast Providence Channel

Bimini Is.
Berry Is.
Spanish Wells
Harbour Island

ATLANTIC

OCEAN

New
Providence
Paradise Is.
NASSAU

Eleuthera

Straits
of
Florida

Great

Andros Is.

Cat I.
▲ Mt. Alvernia
(206ft/63m)

San Salvador

Cay Sal
Bank

Bahama

Exuma Cays

Exuma Sound

Tongue of the Ocean

Rum Cay

Anguilla Cays

Great
Exuma
Little
Exuma
Long I.

Tropic of Cancer

Bank

Samana Cays

Old Bahama Channel

Crooked Island Passage

Crooked I.

Long
Cay

Mayaguana

Acklins
I.

Mayaguana Passage

TURKS &
CAICOS
(U.K.)

Ragged I.

Caicos Passage

Little Inagua

CUBA

Great Inagua

L. Rosa

Windward Passage

DOMINICAN
REPUBLIC

HAITI

when a Canadian, George Benjamin, began exploring the Andros caves. The famous underwater explorer Jacques Cousteau produced television films featuring the blue holes.

Explorations of the blue holes in the 1980s and 1990s have revealed new information. For example, in Grand Bahama, biologist Jill Yager discovered a new order of marine life—*Remipedia*, a crustacean group believed until then to have become extinct 150 million years ago. In Andros, skeletons and artifacts, including a Lucayan canoe believed to be 1,000 years old, were uncovered. In the process of exploration, new subterranean sites were discovered, including Zodiac Caverns and Stargate. Research is being conducted on how bacteria play a part in the formation of the caves. Once the blue holes were sites for diving adventures, but now they have become the frontiers of scientific study and research.

Divers report a strange orange glow in the blue holes of the Bahamas. Scientists have explained that this is caused by the merging of fresh and sea water. Sea water, being heavier, lies beneath fresh water. Where the two layers merge, a layer called halocline forms. Organic matter that sinks through fresh water settles in the halocline layer where bacterial action causes it to break down. The halocline layer has a different chemical composition from the other two layers of water; it is more corrosive and typically orange.

The Hurricane Hole of Paradise Island is a natural haven for luxury yachts.

CLIMATE

The islands of the Bahamas lie in the path of the Gulf Stream, which helps maintain a uniform temperature the whole year round. (The Gulf Stream, a warm ocean current, flows northward from the Gulf of Mexico toward Newfoundland.) Winter lasts from mid-December to mid-April, with an average temperature of 72° F (22° C). Summer (mid-April to mid-December) temperatures rarely exceed 85° F (29° C), since the trade winds blowing off the ocean keep the islands comparatively cool. There is little variation in the mean temperatures from north to south.

The average annual rainfall is 50 inches (130 cm), and relative humidity is 60–90%. The islands usually have only short tropical showers, but for six months, from June to November, Bahamians experience rainier weather: about 80% of the annual rainfall is in those months.

The Bahamas is just outside the Caribbean hurricane belt, and very few hurricanes in the past century have caused any major damage, such as that experienced periodically in Florida. The average incidence of hurricanes for the Bahamas has been once in nine years. The worst hurricane disaster ever recorded in the Bahamas was in 1929, when 140 miles per hour (225 km per hour) winds struck the islands. Many lives were lost, and buildings, homes, and boats were damaged. More recently, in October 1996, Hurricane Lili battered resorts and devastated buildings and an airport tower. Today, with satellite forecasts broadcast over the media, people are generally prepared for really severe storms.

FLORA

The Bahamas contains a significant amount of uncultivated land, due to extensive swamps. Centuries of decay of all kinds of vegetable matter on many of the islands have enriched the soil. As a result, although there is

Above: The yellow elder is the national flower of the Bahamas.

Left: Botanical gardens in the Bahamas such as the Ardastra Gardens and Zoo in Nassau are beautifully landscaped with palms and other tropical plants.

Above: **Monkey or cat tails is a common Bahamian plant.**

Opposite: **A parrot greets visitors to Ardastra Zoo in Nassau.**

little lush vegetation, some of the islands, such as Andros and the Abacos, have forests of mahogany, ironwood, pine, and *lignum vitae*, a hardwood with dark blue flowers considered the Bahamian national tree. The original forests have been logged extensively to support boat-building and construction, as well as to clear land for plantations.

Bahamian plants include palms, ferns, bull vine, and some 30–40 wild orchid species. Mangrove plants, which can tolerate sea water, grow extensively in the swamps. Among plants introduced in the last century are Australian casuarinas; they were imported to prevent the erosion of sand dunes and are now part of the landscape. Fruit trees such as figs, tamarinds, and plums are also cultivated.

FAUNA

The Bahamas has two indigenous terrestrial animals: the raccoon and the hutia, a species of guinea pig. Other animals were introduced over the years, and the wild horses, pigs, and donkeys living on some of the islands are descendants of domestic animals brought in by the early settlers. The Bahamian rock iguana, the Cat Island terrapin, the hawksbill turtle, and the green turtle are some reptiles and amphibians found in the Bahamas.

About 5% of the world's coral reefs are found in the Bahamas, enriching its variety of marine life. Marine biologists are attracted to the Bahamas because its sea water is especially clear, being devoid of the silt carried to the sea by rivers—there are no rivers in the Bahamas. Capitalizing on this, the Wild Dolphin Project was founded in 1985 to study the behavior and social interactions of free-ranging Atlantic dolphins.

The Bahamas is a birdwatcher's paradise. The pink flamingo, the national bird, is found on all the islands, but Great Inagua has a flamingo rookery with over 50,000 birds. Also quite common are roseate spoonbills, green parrots, hummingbirds, and herons. The Bahama parrot is a unique bird that nests in limestone cavities at ground level, making it vulnerable to predators such as wild cats. The Abaco National Park is a protected nesting area and habitat for this endangered species.

Migratory birds include egrets, wild ducks, and wild geese. The islands are their winter home. Frigate birds, also called man-o'-war birds, frequent the Bahamas—airplane pilots have reported seeing these large seabirds flying as high as 8,000 feet (2,440 m)!

PROTECTING WILDLIFE

The Bahamas is a member of CITES, the Convention on International Trade in Endangered Species of Wild Flora and Fauna, which was created in 1973 to protect wildlife against exploitation of species on a scale that threatens its existence. In accordance with CITES rules, the Bahamas has divided its endangered species into two groups: those near extinction and those likely to become endangered. No trade is allowed in the first category, while limited trade is permitted for the second.

Among the species nearing extinction are peregrine falcons, Bahama parrots, four species of turtles (loggerhead, hawksbill, green, and leatherback turtles), Bahamian rock iguanas, American crocodiles, whales, dolphins, and West Indian manatees.

The Ministry of Agriculture is the CITES managing authority in the Bahamas, while the Bahamas National Trust acts as the scientific authority. Together, these organizations grant permits for trade in endangered species and educate people on the need to preserve wildlife, particularly endangered species.

This panoramic view of Nassau shows the bridge linking New Providence and Paradise Island in the distance.

NEW PROVIDENCE

Although it is far from being the biggest island in the Bahamas, New Providence has the largest population, because the capital, Nassau, is located here. West of Nassau lies Cable Beach, one of the best-known coastal resorts in the Bahamas. The name commemorates the first telegraph cable, laid in 1892, linking Jupiter in Florida to the Bahamas. The island has some of the country's major historical sites, but it is mainly the man-made attractions that draw tourists and business people. Nassau International Airport is located in the western half of New Providence.

Just 600 feet (180 m) across a small inlet from the city of Nassau lies the 685 acre (280 hectare) Paradise Island, which originally went by the unromantic name of Hog Island. It was once privately owned; its first owner, William Sayle, bought it for US$294. Paradise Island has been developed as a major resort complex, with many five-star hotels, casinos, and world-class golf courses. About 70% of all visitors to the Bahamas land first on either New Providence or Paradise Island.

NASSAU

Nassau, in the northwest of New Providence, is the government, finance, and tourist center of the Bahamas. It has many architecturally interesting buildings, ranging from Victorian homes built by the British administrators of the islands to modern luxury apartments and resorts. It still retains a British flavor. The capital was founded in 1656 and named by its British rulers for King William III of England, one of whose titles was Prince of Nassau.

Among Nassau's numerous historical sites is the 18th century Fort Charlotte, complete with a moat and dungeons. Another fort, Fort Fincastle, was designed to resemble a paddle-wheel steamer. The fort was converted into a lighthouse because of its location on the highest point of the island. Linking this fort to the Princess Margaret Hospital is the Queen's Staircase, a flight of 66 steps carved out of calcareous sandstone at the end

Above: The Queen's Staircase in Nassau.

Left: The Atlantis hotel complex rises from the sea on Paradise Island, almost like a lost world rediscovered.

of the 18th century. Government House, the official residence of the British governor (today, this is a ceremonial post), is an imposing pink-and-white building. The octagonal building that is the Nassau Public Library and Museum was once the city jail, and its small cells are now lined with bookshelves. One of the oldest buildings in the city, the two-story Vendue House (1769), was originally a single-story slave market. It now houses the Pompey Museum, a cultural museum named to honor a slave who led several uprisings in the 1830s against his colonial masters on the island of Great Exuma. Also of historical significance is the Royal Victoria Gardens, the site of the Royal Victoria Hotel built in expectation of an influx of American tourists. The American Civil War dashed that hope, but it created another kind of boom for the hotel, attracting Confederate officers, Yankee spies, gunrunners, and news reporters. The hotel closed in 1971, and shortly after that it burned down. Its ruins now make a vivid background for landscaped gardens.

The heart of the city is Rawson Square, which lies in the center of Bay Street. Close to the square is one of the largest straw markets in the world, where visitors can see all kinds of items woven from "palmetto," a natural fiber.

Bay Street, the city's main thoroughfare, contains shops that sell anything from duty-free Swiss watches to voodoo dolls and Chinese silk dresses. Bay Street is also the location of the biggest banks. The capital has become a significant offshore banking center in the Caribbean. Many of the world's major banks have outlets in Nassau that offer a wide variety of banking services to wealthy people drawn by the Bahamas' reputation as a tax-free haven.

Behind Bay Street is a wharf complex where cruise liners dock, bringing passengers from all over the world to experience Bahamian hospitality and to buy souvenirs in the Bay Street shops. An interesting range of boats dock at the quays, from huge container ships to the small and often unique mailboats that are lifelines to outlying islands. Given enough time (time on a mailboat is quite flexible), visitors can ride on mailboats to the nearby islands. Horse-drawn carriages known as surreys are a tourist attraction in Nassau. Their drivers—trained tour guides—take visitors around the major attractions of the city.

Above: **Vessels anchored at one of Nassau's many marinas.**

Opposite: **Rawson Square in the heart of Nassau is the location of government offices including the prime minister's office.**

GRAND BAHAMA

Grand Bahama in the north is the fourth largest island in the Bahamian archipelago. The island is about 75 miles (120 km) long and 5–17 miles (8–27 km) wide. The northern shore is covered with mangrove swamps and wetlands; the southern shore is a long stretch of white beaches.

For many centuries Grand Bahama was only visited, but never settled, by colorful characters ranging from Juan Ponce de León in 1513 (looking for the Fountain of Youth) to pirates in the 17th and 18th centuries. The first settlers came to Grand Bahama around 1841, but another century passed before anyone considered serious development there.

In the 1950s, an American, the Virginian lumber baron Wallace Groves, began to take an interest in developing the pine-forested island for commercial use. From these beginnings grew the community of Freeport, which is now a major industrial center for the Bahamas, as well as a tourist center with major hotels, casinos, golf courses, and sport fishing.

The water surrounding Grand Bahama is incredibly clear so the island has become a mecca for divers drawn by the fabulous variety of fish and some interesting shipwrecks. Several national parks are located here, including the Lucayan National Park, a well-charted underwater cave system, the Peterson Cay National Park, and the Rand Nature Center in the heart of Freeport, a birdwatcher's haven with a 2,000-foot (600 m) nature trail through a woods and pine landscape. The curators lead educational birdwatching and wildflower tours every month. UNEXSO (Underwater Explorer's Society) offers a "Dolphin Experience" in Lucaya, where people interact with dolphins.

Observing dolphins at close quarters in Grand Bahama's "Dolphin Experience." The dolphins here are not living in captivity but are free to come and go.

FREEPORT AND LUCAYA

The second major city of the Bahamas after Nassau is Freeport. With its twin city Lucaya, it was created by the rum-runners who made their homes and lucrative businesses there in the 1920s and 1930s, during Prohibition in the United States. By the 1950s, there were still only about 4,000 people living there. Then a deepwater port was built to handle the growing lumber trade on the island. To encourage enterprise in the area, the Bahamian government generously allowed businesses to locate and run their operations there free of tax—hence the name "Freeport."

Freeport has developed and grown tremendously since the 1950s. Together with Lucaya it has now also become the second greatest tourist destination in the country after Nassau. The city is planned on a grid with wide streets and widely separated buildings, giving people the impression that the city is less friendly, less "Bahamian" in character.

THE FAMILY ISLANDS

The Bahamas can be divided into three main regions—New Providence island with the capital Nassau, Grand Bahama, and the appropriately named Out Islands—all the other islands and cays. The government has renamed these the "Family Islands," a name intended to give people a better perception of the islands, one that is inclusive and not unwelcoming.

For centuries, the Family Islanders led a precarious existence through subsistence farming and fishing, their only link with the outside world the mailboat from Nassau. For some of the islands this is still true, although Radio Bahamas now links all the islands and radio-telephone facilities are available on most of them, while islands with larger populations also have their own airports. The Family Islands have their own schools and medical facilities, as well as local government. Many of them are developing their infrastructure to attract some of the lucrative tourist business currently centered on New Providence and Grand Bahama.

THE ABACOS include Great Abaco, Little Abaco, and offshore cays with a 150-year-old reputation for boat-building. In Man-O-War Cay, boats are still handmade. There is an atmosphere of New England in the cays, particularly in New Plymouth and Hope Town, where a style of house called the saltbox is preserved.

ACKLINS AND CROOKED ISLANDS, together with Long Cay, form an atoll enclosing a lagoon. This was once a favorite hideout of pirates, who ambushed ships passing through the Crooked Island Passage. The islands were settled by American Loyalists in the 18th century, but most of them left when their cotton plantations became uneconomical.

ANDROS, the largest island on the Bahamian archipelago, has some of the deepest blue holes. Except for the northeastern coast, where the bigger towns are located, the island is underdeveloped. The Atlantic Undersea Testing and Evaluation Center, a joint operation of the U.S. Navy and the Bahamian government, is located near Fresh Creek and is one of the busiest underwater testing facilities in the world.

BERRY ISLANDS is a group of 30 islands and nearly 100 cays. The islands attract mainly divers and beach lovers.

BIMINI consists of two islands: North Bimini is more populated, while South Bimini is the site of an airport. The legendary Fountain of Youth is supposed to be located in South Bimini, near the airport.

The Compleat Angler is a hotel and a bar as well as an Ernest Hemingway museum. The Nobel Prize-winning writer first stayed here in 1935, and sport fishing in the Biminis is said to have inspired *The Old Man and the Sea.*

CAT ISLAND is the only "highland" in the Bahamas, the country's highest point being Mt. Alvernia. That is the site of a small monastery built by a Jesuit architect, Father Jerome.

ELEUTHERA was settled by English pilgrims in the 17th century. The Eleutherian Adventurers created Dunmore Town on Harbour Island, off northern Eleuthera. Another northern Loyalist settlement, Spanish Wells, is one of the richest Bahamian communities, with wealth from fishing.

THE EXUMAS are 365 cays stretched over 100 miles (160 km). The main islands are Great Exuma and Little Exuma and the principal settlement is George Town. The Exuma National Land and Sea Park is the world's first national park to lie partially submerged.

THE INAGUAS—two islands, Great Inagua and Little Inagua—have a harsh landscape, a hot climate, and little rainfall—all of which helps their major industry of salt production. About 80 salt ponds cover 12,000 acres

BEST BEACHES, GREAT DIVE SITES

The Bahamas have some of the most idyllic beaches in the world. The sand is fine and white and visible beneath shallow, crystal clear water several yards out to sea. With more than 2,000 islands and cays, there are countless beaches to choose from. Among the most populated beaches are Old Fort Beach and Cable Beach in New Providence, Cabbage Beach in Paradise Island, Xanadu Beach in Grand Bahama, Tahiti Beach in the Abacos, Pink Sands Beach in Harbour Island, Ten Bay Beach in Eleuthera, and Saddle Cay in the Exumas. They are filled with opportunities for leisure sports and entertainment—water-skiing, windsurfing, snorkeling, beach bars, and restaurants. About 80% of the Bahamian beaches are practically deserted, making them ideal for those who enjoy nature untouched by human activity and sounds.

The Bahamas is also a year-round diver's dream. There are dive sites for those who like exploring wrecks, but the main attraction is the marine life. Most of the islands are ringed with coral reefs—the reef off Andros is the third largest in the world. Dive sites have imaginative names: the Wall, Theo's Wreck, Spit City, Rose Garden, and Ben Blue Hole are some of them. Current Cut is an underwater gully that carries divers for a 10-minute ride on a swiftly flowing underwater current.

(5,000 hectares). Great Inagua is well known for its brilliant pink flamingos, which are protected in a vast reserve, the Inagua National Park.

LONG ISLAND is aptly named, being 60 miles (97 km) long and only 4 miles (6 km) wide. Loyalist mansions remain, although the plantations are no more. Today the islanders cultivate vegetables and raise livestock.

MAYAGUANA, the easternmost Bahamian island, is secluded and seldom visited except by sport fishing enthusiasts.

SAN SALVADOR was originally named by Christopher Columbus, and is now again so named. It was called Watling Island between 1680 and 1926, after John Watling, a very religious pirate captain.

"Inagua" is an anagram for "iguana," the herbivorous lizard found on Bahamian beaches. However, "inagua" is believed to be derived from the Spanish lleno *(full) and* agua *(water).*

A diet of brine shrimp helps the flamingos of the Bahamas maintain their brilliant pink color.

NATIONAL PARKS—A NATIONAL TRUST

In 1959, to save the West Indian flamingo from extinction, the Bahamas National Trust was created by an act of parliament. As a result, the Exuma Cays Land and Sea Park was established—a 176 square mile (456 square km) marine reserve for tropical birds and the Bahamian iguana. By the end of the millennium, the Trust had created 11 more national parks, covering hundreds of thousands of acres of wetlands and forests, to protect the country's biodiversity and natural resources. As part of its conservation responsibilities, the Trust formulates the national strategy for environment and development, makes recommendations for ecotourism, conducts independent studies of projects such as resort developments that impact on the environment, contributes the environmental component to the national education curriculum, and participates in numerous international conferences on environmental issues.

The national parks run by the Trust protect diverse species and at the same time offer eco-related activities such as birdwatching and nature

24

walks. In the Abacos, a parrot haven was created in the Abaco National Park, while Black Sound Cay is a waterfowl habitat. Conception Island National Park is a sanctuary for migratory birds, a rookery for seabirds, and an egg-laying site for the green turtle. Green turtles also visit the Union Creek Reserve of Great Inagua, a 7 square mile (18 square km) enclosed tidal creek that is a breeding research site for giant sea turtles. Plants are not forgotten. In the middle of Nassau's residential area, the headquarters of the Trust manages 11 acres (4.5 hectares) of botanical gardens and 200 species of palm trees, the largest private collection in the West Indies.

Among the parks, Lucayan National Park in Grand Bahama is special: this is the longest—6 miles (10 km)—charted underwater cave system in the world. Ongoing scientific studies here have contributed to greater understanding of the chemistry of similar limestone caves. Pelican Cays Land and Sea Park in the Abacos is another site known for undersea caves.

Above: **The coral reefs have brilliant marine life such as orange sponge and purple and yellow Royal Gramma.**

Left: **An enterprising tourist company in Nassau offers underwater ecology walks.**

HISTORY

MANY SPECIFIC EVENTS IN HISTORY contribute to our understanding of any country. For the Bahamas, some of these events began elsewhere, for many of the islands were not populated until the original settlers arrived from other islands.

THE LUCAYANS

At least 500 years before the Europeans arrived in the New World, the Bahamas was inhabited by a gentle race of people called the Lucayans ("loo-KAH-yahns"). They were descendants of the Arawak Indians, who originally lived in northern South America, throughout the islands of the Caribbean, and as far north as present-day Florida. The Lucayans had gradually been driven northward by the Carib tribe—a warlike people, whose practice of cannibalism made them very much feared by the peaceable Lucayans. Although the Lucayans had weapons, such as bows and poison-tipped arrows, they had not developed armor to protect themselves.

For centuries, the Lucayans lived a simple life in villages throughout the Bahamas, subsisting mainly on fish caught with bone fishhooks, and growing corn and cassava root for food. They also grew cotton, which they spun and wove into hammocks—these attracted the attention of the first Europeans to visit the Bahamas, as hammocks provided a comfortable alternative to the hard decks of their ships. The Lucayans traveled in big canoes carved out of mahogany logs. One such canoe sunk more than 500 years ago was discovered in an Andros blue hole in the 1990s.

Above: **The Lucayans lived off the sea.**

Opposite: **A lighthouse on San Salvador, the first Bahamian island that Christopher Columbus visited. His arrival put the Bahamas on the map of the civilized world.**

Above: **When Columbus arrived with his crew, the Lucayans welcomed them with food and gifts.**

Opposite: **The Bahamian islands attracted fortune-seekers such as Ponce de León (c. 1460–1521).**

CHRISTOPHER COLUMBUS

On October 12, 1492, Christopher Columbus stepped ashore on a little island that the Lucayans called Guana-hani. He immediately renamed it San Salvador, and claimed it for Spain. The Lucayans welcomed Columbus and his men from whom they saw no threat—initially there was none because the coral islands had no economic value. Columbus was looking for gold and a passage to China.

After some time in the islands, which he later described as being among the most beautiful he had ever seen, Columbus sailed south toward Cuba. His expedition discovered gold on Hispaniola (modern-day Haiti and Dominican Republic). Before the gold was exhausted, however, the Taino natives of Hispaniola died from overwork or foreign diseases against which they had little immunity. Remembering the Lucayans, the Spanish sent an expedition to round them up.

Historians have recorded that about 40,000 Lucayans were either killed for resisting or subdued and shipped to Hispaniola to work. Approximately 25 years after Christopher Columbus discovered San Salvador, Lucayan society in the Bahamas did not exist.

SLEEPING ISLANDS

The Bahamian islands came under the nominal control of Spain after Columbus's visit, an arrangement formalized under the Treaty of Tordesillas between Spain and Portugal in 1494. For more than a century, however, they were seldom visited, much less settled. From time to time explorers would wander into the shallow seas, then move on. One such visitor was Ponce de León, a Spanish conqueror looking for the fabled Fountain of Youth. Other Europeans passed through, including the Dutch and the French. British explorers such as John Cabot and John Hawkins also visited the Bahamas during the 1500s, but they too did not stay. All these explorers were very likely discouraged by the treacherous reefs surrounding many of the islands.

It was not until 1629 that anyone thought seriously about settling the Bahamas. In that year, ignoring the Spanish claim, King Charles I of England granted to his attorney-general, Sir Robert Heath, the right to establish settlements in territories in America including "Bahama" and all the islands lying south or near the continent. This right was never exercised: the islands were too far away, and besides, Charles I had major problems in England, which ended with his execution in 1649. (Robert Heath fled to France.)

Meanwhile, conflict between the Puritans and the Anglican Church in England caused the Puritans to leave for North America and other territories, among them the Bermuda islands, which England had colonized in 1612.

The early travelers faced many dangers in the Bahamas: shipwrecks were a common occurrence.

THE ELEUTHERIAN ADVENTURERS

Old World religious influence soon reached the New World, and in the Bermudas some oppressed Puritans decided it was time to move on. In 1647 William Sayle formed the Company of Eleutherian Adventurers whose goal was to look for an island where they would be free to establish plantations and to worship as they wished. In the summer of 1648, Sayle and 70 other Puritans arrived at Governor's Harbour on the island of Cigatoo, now known as Eleuthera, and became the first group of Europeans to take up residence in the Bahamas.

The newcomers had a rocky start. Even before they arrived, one of their two ships was wrecked. They sent the other ship out for provisions. To survive in the long term, however, they needed more than provisions. Rich soil was necessary for farming, but the island's coralline base was covered by only a thin layer of poor soil. Consequently, many of their farming projects failed. For a few years Sayle traveled in search of funds. Fellow Puritans who had settled in the new colony of Massachusetts on

bug and soil exhaustion. Many settlers eventually emigrated, some to resettle on more fertile British Caribbean islands such as Barbados, others to return to the United States. Those who stayed did quite well for themselves eventually, by branching into other occupations, including fishery and boatbuilding. Remnants of Loyalist communities are still found on the islands, their homes in the architectural styles they brought with them. Several Bahamian family names can be traced to the Loyalist settlers. In the Exumas, for example, many residents are called Rolle after their slave ancestors who adopted the name of their master, Denys Rolle.

The slave population increased to over 12,000 by the start of the 1800s. The social system in the Bahamas began to change in this period, beginning with the abolition of the slave trade throughout the British Empire in 1807 and the total emancipation of slaves in 1834. Indentured labor and universal education were introduced.

The emancipation of slaves in the Bahamas was painless compared with the situation in the American South. This is possibly because the plantations had failed, and slaves were no longer essential; instead their welfare was a financial burden. By the time of the American Civil War, the population of the Bahamas was mostly black.

New Plymouth's jail in Green Turtle Cay is now an attraction for curious visitors. The Loyalists gave their settlements names that reminded them of the homes they had left.

The Royal Victoria Hotel was patronized by a varied and interesting clientele, including journalists, gun-runners, and spies.

BLOCKADE RUNNING

For most of the 19th century the Bahamian islands were tranquil, although not very prosperous owing to few trading opportunities. Most families lived on subsistence farming. The outbreak of the American Civil War in 1861 brought a new activity: blockade running became a very profitable business.

Early in the Civil War, President Lincoln imposed a blockade on the American South to starve it into submission. The Bahamians supplied the Southern states with the manufactured goods they needed but could no longer obtain through the northern ports of the United States, and at the same time marketed the cotton exports of these states in Nassau. Many Bahamians had special fast ships built to make their fortunes evading the gunships of the Yankee army enforcing the blockade. The Royal Victoria Hotel, which had just been built to house an expected influx of American tourists to Nassau, instead became a center for the blockade runners and quickly earned a reputation as the place to party every night.

The excitement and prosperity of the Civil War years ended all too soon with the surrender of the Confederacy in 1865, and the Bahamas returned to its normal, sleepy existence. New opportunities emerged only to fail. For example, conch shells became a good trade item for a while until the fashion for them died. The trade in sponges prospered until they were all killed off by a fungus. Finally, the pineapple-canning factories, which had been established in the Bahamas with high expectations, began to fail after the American government put a punitive import tax on pineapples entering the United States. The citrus fruit crops met the same fate.

PROHIBITION BOOM

As Florida began to develop, many Bahamians left to settle there, with mixed results. On the positive side, new communication links were established with the booming city of Miami—first a regular steamship service, then a telegraph connection, and after 1931, radio links. One negative result was the depletion of the population in the Bahamas.

This time salvation came with the advent of Prohibition in 1919. For the next 14 years the Bahamas supplied illegal alcohol to speakeasies (places selling drinks illegally) all over the United States. The good old days of blockade running began again, and many Bahamians made fortunes operating small, fast boats that outran the U.S. Coast Guard and delivered whisky, gin, rum, and beer to the many inlets dotting the east Florida coast. In 1933 Prohibition ended and the Bahamas succumbed to the Depression, which had already affected people elsewhere.

World War I badly damaged the economy of the islands, still strongly linked to that of Britain. The Bahamas had little real contact with the war, but the people proved themselves to be British patriots by contributing lives and funds to the war effort.

Seated on a heap of sponges, a Bahamian prepares a consignment for export as the sponge trade nears its end in the early 20th century.

The Duchess of Windsor presents a trophy to a Blackhawks polo team member in Nassau as the governor of the Bahamas, the Duke of Windsor, looks on.

A TAX REFUGE

It was a millionaire this time who saved the Bahamas. In 1934, Sir Harry Oakes, who had made his fortune in Canadian goldmines, found the Bahamas a good place to live, both for its climate and for its welcome, hands-off attitude toward the taxes he should be paying on his fortune. He told his friends about this attractive tax haven, and the Bahamas began to gain popularity among the wealthy for permanent residence. Among those who could not afford to live there it became known as a beautiful place to visit.

The appointment of the Duke of Windsor, the former king of England who had abdicated to marry a divorcée, as the governor of the Bahamas in 1940 added to the attraction of the Bahamas during World War II, for the duke was a popular man. He instituted economic reforms and was instrumental in the building of an airbase on New Providence to train pilots during the war. The Bahamas also became important as a strategic base for anti-submarine warfare against the Germans. Two new airports built during the war to support the Allied forces based there later provided the infrastructure for the postwar tourist boom.

After the war ended the Bahamians took advantage of the facilities left behind by the British to develop the tourist industry in a big way. This was timely, for by then the attitude of the middle classes to leisure had changed, and more people who were not rich were traveling for pleasure. Then, in the early 1960s, after Cuba became communist and the United States imposed an embargo on that country, tourists looking for a new destination discovered the perfect alternative in the Bahamas.

INDEPENDENCE

The Bahamians had been in control of their internal government since Woodes Rogers established an assembly of representatives in 1729, but sovereignty was still held by the British Crown. In 1963, during a conference in London, it was agreed that the Bahamas should be given self-government. The process began with a new constitution in 1964 and the first general election to choose a prime minister and cabinet.

In 1967, after the second election, in which the first black prime minister was elected, the Bahamas achieved full self-government, with the United Kingdom retaining control of foreign affairs, defense, and internal security. The Bahamas became fully independent July 10, 1973, when its nominally adopted name of Commonwealth of the Bahama Islands was changed to Commonwealth of the Bahamas.

Bahamian police undergo inspection by their British officers in Nassau.

GOVERNMENT

FOR 250 YEARS the Bahamas was a colony of Great Britain, and all the important decisions affecting the growth of the country and the welfare and taxation of the Bahamian people were made on the other side of the Atlantic Ocean, in London. The governors of the Bahamas enjoyed local authority after 1729, but until recently they were required to refer any major decisions to the British Colonial Office, and through that to the British Parliament.

As late as the early 1950s, there were no political parties in the Bahamas, so Bahamians had no official body to express their concerns and wishes about the way the islands were governed. Twenty years later, however, the Bahamas had become a fully independent, sovereign country, with a government authorized by the electorate to decide on every aspect of government, including foreign relations and defense.

Today, the Bahamas is a parliamentary democracy and a member of the Commonwealth of Nations, a grouping of countries once governed by Great Britain. The British monarch, Queen Elizabeth II, is its head of state, and she is represented by a Bahamian-born governor-general whom she appoints on the advice of the prime minister of the Bahamas.

This chapter examines significant events after World War II and popular attitudes that shaped modern politics in the Bahamas. It also describes the political parties, the present structure of government, the important features of the Bahamian constitution, and organizations that support the functions of government.

Above: **In 1992 Hubert Alexander Ingraham led the Free National Movement to electoral victory and became the prime minister of the Bahamas.**

Opposite: **Government House in Grand Bahama is an ornate building.**

Above: **The changing-of-the-guard ceremony at Government House is performed with pomp and pageantry every other Saturday morning in Nassau.**

Opposite: **The Commonwealth secretary, George Thomson, addresses the Bahamas Constitutional Conference in London, while Lynden Pindling, the prime minister of the Bahamas, seated opposite, listens attentively.**

POSTWAR POLITICAL CHANGES

Long before World War II, the political assembly had been in the hands of the white merchants and lawyers known as the Bay Street Boys. The term was derogatory, for this group was blamed for practically everything that went wrong in the Bahamian economy. The blacks had been overlooked as a political force by the Bay Street group. But during the war, thousands of blacks lost their lives, a point that some of them drove home to their countrymen. This was the beginning of a shift in the political power base.

In 1953 the Progressive Liberal Party (PLP) was founded by a group led by Lynden O. Pindling, with a political platform of improving the social, economic, and political situation in the Bahamas. The Bay Street Boys reacted to this by forming the United Bahamian Party (UBP) in 1958. Britain sent the secretary of state for the colonies to the Bahamas to determine the grassroots political sentiment, and as a result of his recommendations, the 1960s was a time of great political change in the Bahamas.

In 1964 a new Bahamian constitution was adopted, the first-ever specifically for the Bahamas itself. It replaced the colonial government structure with a two-chamber house of assembly elected by Bahamians and headed by a prime minister and a cabinet whose members were drawn from the political party with the most votes. The British Parliament continued to appoint a governor to look after British interests in the Bahamas, but now he acted only in consultation with the prime minister.

The UBP, led by Roland Symonette, won the first election by a narrow majority. The opposition in parliament, led by Lynden Pindling, adopted a political strategy of disobedience in parliament that climaxed in their boycott of parliament in 1967. This forced another election, and Pindling became the first black prime minister of the Bahamas.

He began the process of leading the country toward total independence from Great Britain. In 1969 changes to the constitution gave the Bahamas self-government, and only defense, foreign relations, and internal security remained with the British government.

Not all the Bahamians wanted independence. Many felt there was no need to hurry the process, among them the Free National Movement (FNM), a 1971 coalition of the UBP and dissident members of the PLP. By majority vote, however, the electorate decided the issue when they elected Pindling again for a second term in 1972.

A constitutional conference was called in London to discuss the proposal for total independence. As a result of the London talks a new constitution for the Bahamas was drawn up. At midnight on July 9, 1973, the birth of the new independent nation of the Bahamas was symbolically recognized by the lowering of the Union Jack and the raising of the new Bahamian flag.

A Bahamian policeman directs traffic.

THE CONSTITUTION

The 1973 constitution of the Bahamas came into effect when the Commonwealth of the Bahamas became an independent nation. It proclaims the Bahamas to be a sovereign democratic state, establishes the executive, legislative, and judicial branches of government, and creates the Public Service Commission, the Judicial and Legal Commission, and the Police Service Commission. The constitution guarantees fundamental rights and freedoms and the protection of these rights under the law without discrimination based on race, national origin, political opinion, color, creed, or gender. The constitution may be amended only by an act of parliament in combination with a popular referendum.

GOVERNMENT STRUCTURE

The governor-general appointed by the British monarch plays a ceremonial role. The actual business of governing is conducted by the Bahamian Parliament. This body has two chambers—the Senate and the House of Assembly. The Senate has 16 members appointed by the governor-general: nine on the advice of the prime minister, four on the advice of the leader of the opposition, and three on the advice of the prime minister after consultation with the leader of the opposition. The House of Assembly is composed of at least 38 members elected in democratic elections (the legal voting age is 18) at least every five years. The number of assembly members may be increased by the Constituencies Commission, which reviews electoral boundaries every five years. The election of 1997 created a house of 40 members, a decrease in the number of seats from 49. The executive branch of government is the cabinet of at least nine ministers appointed by the prime minister. The cabinet includes the prime minister and the attorney-general.

The constitution requires laws to be enacted by parliament in a certain manner: a bill is introduced in the House of Assembly, read three times, and debated. If it is passed, it becomes an act. The act is read three times in the Senate and then sent to the governor-general. When he has signed the act, it is published in the official journal of the government and becomes a law.

THE JUSTICE SYSTEM

The justice system is modeled on the British common law system but includes Bahamian statute law. Many members of the legal profession in the Bahamas have trained in and are eligible to practice in England. The judiciary is independent of government control.

The hierarchy of courts ranges from local magistrates' courts in New Providence and Grand Bahama to the Supreme Court (one each in Nassau and Freeport) and the Court of Appeal. There is also the right of appeal to Her Majesty's Privy Council in England.

Appeals move upward; for example, an appeal from a decision of a Family Island commissioner is heard in a magistrate's court, while an appeal from a decision in a magistrate's court is heard in the Supreme Court. The Bahamian justice system is constantly reviewed by the attorney-general and the Bahamas Bar Association.

The Supreme Court (the one above is in Nassau) is presided over by the chief justice or one of seven other justices appointed by the governor-general.

GOVERNMENT LEADERS

Lynden O. Pindling (1930–) from south Andros was the prime minister of the Bahamas from 1967 to 1992. He made history in 1967 by becoming the first black Bahamian prime minister, leading the Progressive Liberal Party to victory against the United Bahamian Party. Pindling led the country to full independence and instituted reforms that transformed banking and investment management into major industries. In 1983 he was knighted Sir Lynden O. Pindling by Queen Elizabeth II. From the 1980s, however, his government was the target of allegations of corruption, particularly of accepting bribes from drug syndicates and improper loans from businessmen. These charges, added to the country's high inflation and unemployment, led to the defeat of his party in the 1992 election. In 1997, after the landslide victory of the Free National Movement party, Pindling resigned as leader of the PLP.

Hubert Alexander Ingraham (1947–) grew up in Cooper's Town on Great Abaco. He qualified as a lawyer in 1972. In 1975 he entered politics as a member of the ruling Progressive Liberal Party, and was elected to the House of Assembly in 1977. After his reelection in 1982 he became the Minister of Housing, National Insurance, and Social Services. Two years later he was dismissed from the cabinet when he protested against government corruption, and in 1986 he was expelled from the party altogether. In the 1987 general election Ingraham ran as an independent candidate and was elected to the House of Assembly. He joined the official opposition to the PLP in April 1990 and was appointed leader of the opposition in May. Ingraham revitalized the Free National Movement, and in 1992 led his party to an overwhelming victory over the PLP, ending their 25-year control of the Bahamian government. He was reelected in 1997 with an even larger majority vote. Besides being the prime minister, Ingraham is also responsible for trade and industry. He has pledged to stamp out all corruption in the Bahamas and to conduct government affairs "in the sunshine."

Opposite: **Royal Bahamas Defense Force officers maintain a semi-military presence on the islands.**

DEFENSE AND POLICE FORCES

The Bahamas has no army or navy. Its Royal Bahamas Defense Force performs mainly the duties of a coast guard service. It has the extremely difficult task of intercepting smugglers who operate in the waters surrounding the islands. The Royal Bahamas Police Force is responsible for the maintenance of law and order everywhere in the Bahamas.

LEADERSHIP CHANGES

Lynden Pindling was prime minister from 1967 until 1992, leading the Progressive Liberal Party. Toward the end of his last term in office, Bahamians were growing increasingly unhappy with his government's corrupt practices. Not surprisingly, the Free National Movement was voted into power in 1992, led by Hubert Ingraham. The FNM majority in 1992 was a slender 56%. The 1997 election saw a significant increase to 85%, for by then it was clear the FNM's policies were helping the country recover after 25 years of mismanagement. Although Pindling won a seat, he retired from politics after the election, and the PLP is now led by Perry Christie. The other opposition party is the Vanguard Nationalist and Socialist Party (VNSP).

To reduce the US$1.1 billion national debt it inherited, the FNM offered an attractive incentive package to foreign investors and home owners. The National Investment Policy encouraged the privatization of government-run businesses to reduce the government's financial burden. With prudent policies, the debt was reduced to US$358 million by 1996, inflation was brought down from 3% in 1985 to 0.5% in 1997, and unemployment—17–22% in the mid-1980s—was reduced to around 10% by 1997.

ECONOMY

AS A HIGH-INCOME COUNTRY, the Bahamas has been disqualified from receiving World Bank loans since 1988. The average annual income per Bahamian was US$11,940 in 1995. Over the years, many different products have earned income for the Bahamas, ranging from pineapples to services, but the country has always been a much larger importer than exporter—over 90% of all its goods are imported, mainly from the United States, Canada, and the United Kingdom.

Today the economy of the Bahamas is less dependent on trade than it used to be. The traffic of people and money through the tourism and banking industries are by far the largest foreign exchange earners. Diversification has been the policy since the early 1970s, because the main industry—tourism—was too dependent on the U.S. economy, the source of most of the tourist dollars. Privatization of former government-run companies is part of the government's economic strategy. This has encouraged home ownership by foreigners, creating a construction boom, and even the sale of islands.

Christopher Columbus said of the Bahamas that "the beauty of these islands surpasses that of any other and as much as the day surpasses the night in splendor." Not surprisingly, the Bahamas is a favorite tourist destination for Americans and Europeans.

Opposite: **A vendor displays her straw wares to advantage.**

Left: **A seaplane takes off from one of the Bimini islands.**

Bargains galore await tourists at the Straw Market in Nassau.

TOURISM

"It's better in the Bahamas" is a slogan of the Ministry of Tourism. The main engine of the Bahamian economy is tourism, which accounts for more than 70% of the national income and directly and indirectly employs about 60% of the labor force. The tourism ministry, one of the most effective in the world, has offices in the United States, Canada, and Europe to market the Bahamas as a tourist destination. More than 80% of tourist arrivals are from the United States.

Tourism has been a major thrust for the government since the Royal Victoria Hotel was built in Nassau to attract American tourists in the mid-19th century, but it was only after World War II ended that government efforts to promote tourism increased significantly. New Providence is the main tourist destination and has seen many hotel and casino developments, particularly in the last decade. One of the biggest resorts, the Atlantis on Paradise Island, which is linked to Nassau by twin bridges, is expected to turn Nassau into the Monte Carlo of the Caribbean.

Similar but smaller-scale tourism developments are taking place on some of the other Bahamian islands in an effort to attract more foreign tourists, especially during the winter months. The town of Freeport on Grand Bahama is being developed into a major tourism and business center through large investments by the Hong Kong-based Hutchinson-Whampoa group, while entrepreneurs are investing heavily in tourism infrastructure on the Family Islands of Eleuthera and Abaco.

BANKING

The other major people-centered economic activity in the Bahamas is banking, which employs 25% of the labor force. The Bahamas has been a well-known international tax haven for about 50 years, and as a result, some of the world's wealthiest citizens have made their homes there. Among the country's attractions are its political stability, generous tax laws (there is no tax in the Bahamas on income, profits, or inheritance), and the ease with which people can reinvest their money. Many foreign banks have been attracted to the Bahamas for the same reason; Bay Street in the center of downtown Nassau has one of the largest concentrations of international banks in the world—giving it the nickname "Little Switzerland." With the passage of financial legislation in the 1990s and the government's creation of the Bahamas Financial Services Secretariat to help foreign individuals and financial institutions use the Bahamas as a major center for international investment, the banking sector is expected to grow tremendously in the 21st century.

The entrance of the Bahamas Financial Centre welcomes visitors with a colorful parade of flags. The Bahamian flag flies between the Union Jack of the United Kingdom and the American Stars and Stripes.

51

A consignment of bananas in Dunmore Town (Eleuthera) harbor, awaiting transport.

MANUFACTURING

Activity in the manufacturing sector is relatively small compared to tourism and banking, employing only 10% of the labor force, but there are some new developments. Near Freeport on Grand Bahama, a major oil refinery and transshipment terminal is being expanded, and there are also plants manufacturing and exporting pharmaceutical products and other chemicals.

Aragonite mining near the Bimini islands and sea-salt refining by solar evaporation on Great Inagua provide more export products for the Bahamas. Locally produced rum is also exported.

AGRICULTURE AND FISHERIES

Agriculture provides a relatively small income for the Bahamas, with exports that include pineapples, bananas, and different varieties of citrus fruit. Most of the farms are small, producing poultry, fruit, and vegetables for local consumption. A World Bank study in 1986 estimated that only 10% of the islands' cultivable land was being worked, and that the Bahamas could be more self-sufficient in food if suitable land on Great Abaco, Andros, and Grand Bahama was developed. Fish farming is encouraged by the government, and seafood products such as crayfish and shrimp are processed for export.

TRADE

The Bahamas' main exports are pharmaceuticals, cement, rum, crayfish, refined chemical products, salt, and aragonite. Major imports are foodstuffs,

manufactured goods, crude oil, automobiles, and electronic products. The country's most important trading partner is the United States. Other trading partners include Spain, the United Kingdom, Norway, France, Italy, Finland, Iran, and Denmark. The Bahamas has an increasing trade deficit because its imports have a much greater value than its exports: in 1996, exports were US$273 million compared with imports at US$1.26 billion. The imbalance is caused partly by the need to import building materials for the construction boom.

The Bahamas is a member of several trade organizations, including the Association of Caribbean States, the U.S.-linked Caribbean Basin Initiative, CARIBCAN (Caribbean and Canada Investment and Industrial Cooperation), Free Trade Area of the Americas, and the Organization of American States. NAFTA (North American Free Trade Agreement), a free trade arrangement between the United States, Canada, and Mexico, has had a negative impact on the Bahamas, as it has had on other Caribbean countries, by excluding the islands from preferential trading terms.

Nassau harbor is a busy port that services luxury cruise liners and other ships.

SHIPPING

Legislation for ship registration was passed in 1976, but a decade later fewer than 400 vessels had been registered. Today, however, the Bahamas is a leading world shipping registry, with more than 1,500 ships registered. The Bahamas Maritime Authority, a semigovernmental organization created in 1995, provides administrative services to ship owners. A cruise ship terminal in Nassau and a container transshipment port opened in 1997 in Freeport are expected to increase revenue from shipping.

TRANSPORTATION

The international airports are in Nassau, Freeport, and Paradise Island. Bahamasair, the national airline, provides flights to these airports from adjacent countries as well as domestic service to some 50 small airports or airstrips on the islands. Most people entering the Bahamas do so through Miami, Florida. The main seaports are Nassau on New Providence, Freeport on Grand Bahama, and Matthew Town on Great Inagua.

The major islands have a good system of roads. Driving is on the left side of the road, unlike in America and Continental Europe. Most of the major islands have a bus service, and minibuses called jitneys travel to the main settlements. Taxis, which are plentiful, are often shared by several people traveling in the same general direction. Taxis come in many shapes and sizes, from small compact cars to minivans and even limousines.

As the Bahamas is an island nation, transportation by boat is important. For many years, mailboats, so-called because they carry mail, have provided links between the major centers and the less inhabited islands, and this is still true today. At any given time, several of these boats of different sizes can be seen berthed at Potter's Quay in Nassau, being loaded with supplies and mail for the small communities that they regularly visit. Mailboats also carry passengers to their ports of call. This mode of travel is not for those on a tight timetable, as the mailboats only follow a rough schedule that can change along the way, and a round trip may take anything from two or three days to a week, depending on the amount of cargo to be loaded and unloaded and the sea conditions.

Goods and people await the unloading of an inter-island mailboat.

The postmaster waits for the mailboat at the post office on Great Exuma.

TELECOMMUNICATION

BaTelCo (Bahamas Telecommunications Corporation), the telecoms authority, was privatized in 1998. All the major islands have automatic telephone systems, including a mobile phone service. As of 1996, there were 334 main telephone lines for every 1,000 people in the Bahamas.

WORKING LIFE

Estimates place the total labor force in the Bahamas at about 150,000, but since many Bahamians on the Family Islands are self-employed fishers and farmers, this statistic may not accurately reflect the actual number of working Bahamians. Of those Bahamians who work for employers, 40% are in the tourism industry, while 30% work for the government in one way or another. About 10% are involved in business services and the private banking industry, while an estimated 5% work in the agricultural sector. The unemployment rate is 10%, while the public sector minimum wage is US$4.12 per hour.

For the majority of Bahamians who work in the tourism industry, working hours are often irregular or on a shift basis; others enjoy normal business hours from Monday to Friday. Business offices do not open on Saturdays, although most stores do. Nothing much is open on Sunday as going to church takes precedence, followed by relaxing.

A lighthouse keeper adjusts the kerosene lamp inside a six-foot (2 m) high fresnel lens, which is typically used in lighthouses, as its total effect is to concentrate light.

ECONOMIC DIRECTION BEYOND 2000

Drug trafficking and smuggling are urgent economic concerns, for the islands are widely scattered, with numerous cays for concealing illegal traffic. The problem is aggravated by the location of the Bahamas between the Americas. It is estimated that more than 90% of the cocaine consumed in the United States comes through the Bahamas.

The economic reforms begun by the government have brought diversification, privatization, and increased foreign investments. To protect these gains made in the last decade, the government expects to make greater efforts to fight crime and corruption in the islands.

THE BAHAMIANS

THERE ARE NO DESCENDANTS in the Bahamas of the first people to ever inhabit any of these islands—the Lucayans disappeared several centuries ago.

Many Bahamian families trace their ancestry back to the colonizing Eleutherian Adventurers who came with Captain William Sayle, seeking religious freedom by settling on the island of Eleuthera in 1647; to the Loyalists who migrated to the Bahamas after the American War of Independence; and to the American Southerners who came just before and during the American Civil War. All of these people brought their slaves, who eventually became the majority component of the Bahamian population.

There are Bahamians who claim as ancestors some of the more notorious pirates who made the Bahamas their home in the 17th century.

THE "TRUE TRUE" BAHAMIAN

There are many definitions of what a "true true" Bahamian actually is, and they all differ, but there is one thing that all Bahamians have in common—no matter how they originally came to the Bahamas (some of them unwillingly), none of them now would live anywhere but in the Bahamas.

Interestingly enough, considering the racial divisiveness in many other parts of the world, even though Bahamians are fairly obviously divided by color, ethnic origin is not a major issue in the Bahamas. Peaceful coexistence has been a way of life in the Bahamas for many generations and racial conflict is very rare.

Above: **"True true" Bahamians can be black or white.**

Opposite: **An Exumian, as those living on the Exuma islands are called. Many Exumians have the surname "Rolle."**

BLACK BAHAMIANS

Approximately 85% of the Bahamian population are descended from migrants who came directly or indirectly from the African continent. Many of them were slaves who migrated in the early 1800s, after the American Revolution, with their British Loyalist owners to work the plantations on the islands. The plantations failed. Not long after slavery was abolished and the slaves were emancipated, but their descendants stayed on in the Bahamas to become the backbone of its citizenry. Not all black Bahamians are descendants of slaves; some are descendants of free property owners who were highly respected in their community.

Although black Bahamians are today thoroughly modern, many vestiges remain of the old ancestry, including the superstitions that many Bahamians hold in spite of their education. Their friendliness and warmth with perfect strangers is another characteristic. Above all, the black Bahamian loves to talk, to anyone and about anything, although politics and sports tend to be favorite topics. It is not unusual to walk down the street in a Bahamian town and fall into earnest conversation with a total stranger, and become fast friends very quickly. By the same token, Bahamians are a very helpful people. If they see people who are clearly not local wandering around as though lost and in need of help, they will quickly overwhelm them with directions and advice—but first, they will probably want to know where these strangers came from, how they liked the Bahamas, and who their parents are.

The gregariousness of black Bahamians extends to their large and extended families. A Bahamian family gathering, which happens during most public holidays, might well include grandparents, parents, children, and first, second, and even third and fourth cousins. Often, all that is needed to be included in a family gathering is a common origin, such as having been born on the same island. Common interests, such as enjoyment of similar food and conversation, also give Bahamians the right to membership in a "family" group.

The disadvantage of this inclusiveness is that in any social circle everyone tends to know everyone else's business. Not that Bahamians are nosey, but they do like to gossip, and for this

An islander in braids.

reason it is hard to keep secret anything that has the slightest tinge of scandal. The gossip is not usually malicious; in a society where nearly everyone is related to someone else, plain curiosity is often the only motive.

"Laid back" is another characteristic that may be applied with some truth to most black Bahamians. This is rooted not in laziness but in an attitude that suggests there is no hurry—why rush to do today something that can well be put off until tomorrow, or better still, next week? It is all a matter of priorities: many of them believe enjoying life in the present is more important than the promise of the rewards that might accrue later through doing something "right now."

For all their outgoing and welcoming nature, black Bahamians are quite shy. Eye contact during conversation is rare, and getting past a casual friendship might take some time.

POPULATION STATISTICS

Population of the Bahamas: 284,000 (1999 estimate)

Age structure: 0–14 years, 28%; 15–64 years, 67%; 65 and over, 5%

Voting age: 18 years

Ethnic composition: blacks 85%, whites 12%, Asians and others 3%

Religions: Baptists 32%, Anglicans 20%, Roman Catholics 19%, Methodists 6%, Church of God) 6%, other Protestants 12%, others 5%

Literacy: 95%

Languages: English, Creole (among Haitians)

Birth rate: 21 per 1,000

Death rate: 5.4 per 1,000

Life expectancy at birth: men 70 years, women 77 years

WHITE BAHAMIANS

The white Bahamians tend to have come from Britain or the United States. Often they are better-educated than the average black Bahamian, many of them holding better jobs and owning finer houses. Today, however, this is not a cause of tension. Bahamians have come a long way since the era of the Bay Street Boys, the all-white oligarchy of merchants and professionals.

White Bahamians do have a different behavior and outlook from their black counterparts. Bahamians of British origin still tend to preserve their privacy by keeping very much to themselves, to a much greater extent than black Bahamians would ever think of doing. White American Bahamians are more outgoing, but they are equally unlikely to have strong personal friendships among the black community.

Bahamians trace their roots by their names: Gibsons are from Scotland; Alburys, Malones, and Russels are descended from Irish Loyalists; and Rolles took their name from Lord Rolle, a wealthy planter who gave his land to his former slaves.

Children in Hope Town, Elbow Cay. Hope Town is populated mostly by the descendants of Loyalist settlers, but many residents in Elbow Cay are in fact foreigners who have bought property there.

A Conchy Joe is likely to be of mixed ethnic descent.

"CONCHY JOES"

"Conchy Joe" is a slang term applied to anyone of Caucasian descent whose family has been in the Bahamas for as long as anyone can remember. They are neither wholly black nor white. Countless Conchy Joe families are now racially mixed, but the typical Conchy Joe is predominantly fair-skinned, often with blue eyes and fair hair.

Conchy Joes tend to stand out from both the black and white Bahamians through their enjoyment of ostentatious possessions and behavior. In fact, being a Conchy Joe is something to advertise for Bahamians who can genuinely claim membership in that clan. Men who belong to this group are reputed to have a flattering manner with women, but also to expect them to be conservative in their behavior.

HAITIANS

There are an increasing number of Haitian migrants now living in the Bahamas, particularly in the major cities where they form much of the manual labor force. Many Haitians originally came to the Bahamas as illegal workers, the majority having left Haiti in recent years to escape poverty and political repression. Haiti is one of the poorest Caribbean countries, while the Bahamas is the richest country between the Americas.

Haitians are mainly French Creole speakers and live in communities of their own, usually in the very poorest neighborhoods. Shorter and darker-skinned than most Bahamians, the majority of this recent migrant population have not received much education. Both white and black Bahamians tend to look down on them, and some resent the Haitians for "stealing" jobs—even though these jobs (such as gardening, domestic work, and cleaning) are usually not ones that the Bahamians want for themselves.

There are approximately 35,000 Haitians living in the Bahamas legally, under the terms of a 1985 treaty between the Bahamas and Haiti that recognized the status of Haitians who arrived without documents prior to 1981. Those who arrived later are detained at a center together with other illegal migrants from Cuba, the Dominican Republic, and other countries until they can be repatriated. About 90% of those detained are Haitians.

Members of the Haitian community have complained of being accosted by the police in public places or visited at home by immigration and police officers and hauled to the detention center as illegals. Unfortunately, the presence of the Haitian community has given rise to social, economic, and political tension in an otherwise easygoing society.

Chinese immigrants bring their culinary traditions with them, adding to the flavors of Bahamian cuisine.

MINORITIES

Chinese, Hispanics, Greeks, and Jews make up about 3% of the population. Many of them arrived in the early 20th century from the United States, Hong Kong, and surrounding islands. They tend to interact within their own communities rather than with other Bahamians.

A family in their Sunday best.

BAHAMIAN DRESS

The proximity of the Bahamas to the United States means that American influence is very strong on the islands. There is little difference between the attitude to fashion in Miami and in Nassau, except perhaps for a certain island flair.

Designer clothes are all the rage in the Bahamas, despite their high cost due to import taxes, and these are what Bahamians wear on the street—the flashier the better. Bahamians have a very exuberant color sense and this is reflected in the combination of clothes they wear. Their taste for vivid colors is also applied to Bahamian houses, which can be painted in every known shade.

As religion is a very important aspect of Bahamian life, most Bahamians also possess an extensive Sunday wardrobe of "church" clothes. The hats worn by women are particularly important items of church attire, and proper shoes must be worn by all, with socks or stockings.

Many Bahamians also have a good knowledge of and interest in the ceremonial dress worn by their African ancestors—including the Ibo, Mandingo, Yoruba, and Congo tribes. However, they very rarely wear African-style clothing, except on very special occasions.

Teachers like these are suitable candidates to match with foreigners in the government's People-to-People program.

Hair is important to a Bahamian, especially for women. No amount of attention to grooming, braiding, perming, straightening, or tinting is too much to achieve just the right result.

PEOPLE-TO-PEOPLE

One of the best ways for visitors to get to know the Bahamas and Bahamians is through the government-sponsored "People-to-People" program. Through this program, run by the Ministry of Tourism, tourists and business people are matched by age, interests, and profession with Bahamian individuals or families, and spend some time in their company during their stay on the islands. This contact can be as simple as having a meal together or as long as spending several days learning about the country and its attractions. Bahamians are by nature friendly and outgoing, and this opportunity to understand them in their own environment often results in long-term friendship.

As part of the program, the People-to-People coordinator organizes a monthly tea party hosted by the governor-general's wife at Government House, the residence of the governor-general. Related programs target foreign students studying in Bahamian colleges, penpals, and the spouses of delegates attending conferences.

LIFESTYLE

HAVING FUN is an integral part of the Bahamian lifestyle, and everything they do generally includes this element—whether at work or at home, enjoying life in the present is often more important than trying to reach the top or making a lot of money.

One consequence is that there is very little sense of urgency in the Bahamas, and the general attitude about time reflects this. Although events that are scheduled to happen at a particular time usually do (store opening hours, for instance), other indicated times can be merely approximate, especially outside the major cities. Taking a dinner invitation for 7:30 p.m. too literally, for example, could cause a guest to arrive at least an hour before the host is ready to receive anyone. When a mailboat captain announces that his boat will depart at 10 p.m., it probably will leave sometime that night when everything has been loaded, but the chances of leaving exactly at 10 p.m. would be extremely slight.

Left: **Urban women in conversation.**

Opposite: **A typical single-story house with gables in Hope Town.**

Neighboring houses in an island settlement.

URBAN VERSUS RURAL

The Bahamian islands have different settlement patterns and degrees of development. The infrastructure—roads, housing, and even golf courses—of any island usually depends on investment by development companies that reap profits from sales of houses and condominiums to foreigners and vacationers. San Salvador, for example, is a Family Island that was well developed in various periods: first in the 1930s, when the entrepreneur Harry Oakes built a hotel (it failed); then in the 1950s and 1960s when the U.S. Navy (using the hotel building as a base), ran a submarine and missile tracking operation; then from the late 1970s onward when home and leisure developers realized the potential of the island for residents and vacationers. A Club Med opened there in 1992.

About 80% of Bahamians live in urban areas, where a sense of urgency promotes efficient functioning. This is generally nonexistent in rural areas including many Family Islands, where the rhythm of life often proceeds at much the same pace as it always has—in harmony with the seasons and the hours of daylight and darkness. Whereas urban dwellers tend to live in orderly communities characterized by a logical system of addresses and some uniformity in housing styles, home to a rural Bahamian can mean almost anything from a newly constructed brick house to a tin shack, and these are not necessarily built along a named road. Bahamians are generally proud of where they live and of their community, often using it as part of their identity when describing themselves. They have no natural preference for town living, and many urban Bahamians confess to envy those who live less hectic lives on the less-inhabited islands.

HOUSING

The majority of Bahamians live in small houses, but what they lack in size, they more than make up for in color—it is not unusual to see an orange house with a purple interior, for instance, or grand ornamentation inside or outside the house.

There are some architecturally outstanding homes in the Bahamas, particularly in Nassau and Freeport, many of them located in quite exclusive residential districts. These Bahamian houses are built in the characteristic "island" style, with covered porches, shaded balconies all around on both stories, sundecks or gables, shuttered windows, and several doors. The interiors are graciously decorated. Outdoors they typically have a lush garden, carefully landscaped and tended. In Loyalist settlements, one still sees old mansions and houses in the New England style. Whatever the size, style, or color of their house, Bahamians are very house-proud and hospitable. An invitation to a meal or simply to "set awhile" and talk is not uncommon.

A double-story brick and timber house in Cat Island.

THE ROLE OF THE FAMILY

Bahamians have a strong, fundamental belief in the value of the family. Many Bahamians come from quite large families. This is especially true of the black Bahamian community, where extended families that include cousins many times removed support each other financially as well as in finding work and negotiating settlements whenever family differences threaten to disrupt the peace and stability of the group.

Bahamians have great respect for their elders. Grandfathers and grandmothers often continue to live with one of their children and are important influences in the raising of their grandchildren. It is now more common than it used to be for both parents to work outside the home, making the role of the grandparents even more important.

The traditional roles of parents in a Western country are also the norm in the Bahamas—the father is the head of the family and the disciplinarian, while the mother concerns herself more with the domestic needs of the family—cooking, housecleaning, doing laundry, and looking after the children's welfare, even if she also works outside the home. Grown children usually continue to live at home until they have completed their education, and often until they marry.

BAHAMIAN WOMEN

Women in parliament include Janet Bostwick, the Minister of Foreign Affairs; Ivy Dumont, the Minister of Education and of Youth, Sports, and Culture; and Theresa Moxey-Ingraham, the Minister of Labor, Immigration, and Training. While the government respects the rights of women, the constitution and the law discriminate against them. Unlike men, women cannot transmit Bahamian citizenship to foreign-born spouses. Where no will exists, possessions of the dead pass to the oldest living male relative.

Violence against women is a serious problem. A private, government-aided crisis center runs a public awareness campaign on domestic violence, and a domestic court presides over family matters such as legal separation, maintenance payments, and court orders to protect women against abusive partners.

The government provides a toll-free hot line with trained counsellors on line for each inhabited island. These volunteers counsel women suffering from abuse at home.

Left: **Janet Bostwick receives a call from Liu Shanzai, the Chinese Vice-Minister of Trade and Economic Cooperation. The head of the Bureau of Women's Affairs, Ms. Bostwick is a strong advocate for human rights, particularly those of women.**

Opposite: **A nearly evenly matched piggyback race.**

73

Song lyrics and myths are traditionally used to teach morals to Bahamian children.
On these islands, the children are raised with much love, but are taught to be disciplined.

A Bahamian mother goes through many rituals to ensure that she has a healthy child.

COMING INTO THE WORLD

Many Bahamians are staunch Christians, so the Bahamian life cycle tends to be dominated by the customs of the Christian Church. At the same time, the African heritage of many Bahamians is still evident. For instance, a new child will almost always be christened in a formal ceremony in church with all the family in attendance. Godparents are often appointed to look after the child's spiritual welfare in the years to come. Even before their official appointment, however, a black cord is likely to have been tied around the newborn's wrist to guard against the entry of evil spirits into the unchristened body, and a Bible might even have been placed at the head of the crib to strengthen this protection. A traditionally superstitious new mother also carefully avoids walking over "grave dirt" or it may take her a long time to recover from the effects of childbirth!

In the Bahamas a christening is a good excuse for a party. The men of the family will often get together after the church ceremony to wet the baby's head—especially if it is a boy!

THE WEDDING

Weddings in the Bahamas have taken place under almost all imaginable circumstances. The knot can be tied in conventional fashion in a historic church, under palm trees on one of a few thousand deserted tropical islands, in a privately chartered yacht, or even underwater with scuba gear. The more exotic weddings, however, are for the tourists. It is only necessary for a couple to be in the Bahamas for as little as three days—at the marriage registrar's discretion—to be married; in normal circumstances, the period of residence is 15 days.

The "true true" Bahamian is likely to be more traditional. "Pomp and circumstance" best describes the Bahamian wedding. Money is almost no object for any Bahamian bride—this is her day and everyone must be reminded of it. Before the wedding the designs of the bride's and

An island couple.

bridesmaids' gowns are extremely important and no effort is spared to make the bridal entourage as spectacular as possible. During the ceremony, music plays an important part (as it does in all Bahamian celebrations), and the wedding march will almost always be heard in a church. After the ceremony, the reception is as lavish as the bride's parents can afford, complete with music and entertainment, speeches, and the ritual throwing of the bridal bouquet into the crowd on the couple's departure.

Long after a loved one has gone, parties may be held to mark his or her death anniversary.

THE FUNERAL

If a wedding is an important social event, a funeral is not less so. The death of a loved one is usually a very sad occasion, but "true true" Bahamians go out of their way to make the sendoff for relatives and friends memorable. Obituaries published in the newspapers describe the deceased in glowing terms and invite all acquaintances to pay their respects.

They can attend the wake, an occasion for all who knew the deceased to gather and talk about his or her life, from time to time refreshing themselves with generous amounts of alcoholic beverages. Wakes often begin in the evening and last all night, ending with a Mass conducted in church. Then the coffin is carried in a procession to the cemetery, to the accompaniment of music, perhaps from a brass band. The usual form is an outward show of grief through tears and the singing of dirges.

Graves adorned with fresh flowers in New Plymouth, Green Turtle Cay.

EDUCATION

Up to the mid-19th century, education in the Bahamas was provided only to the children of well-to-do white families, and selectively to academically able nonwhites, mainly through church-funded schools. Those who could afford an overseas education sent their children to schools in the United States, Canada, and Britain. Public education from the late 19th to the early 20th century was provided by Christian missionary schools.

Today school attendance is universal throughout the Bahamas. There are more than 200 schools, the majority of which are funded and run by the government through the Ministry of Education. They coexist with private schools founded by the various religious orders.

The literacy rate in the Bahamas is approximately 95%, which rivals that of developed countries and is considerably higher than the rate in most countries in the Third World. Education is compulsory from ages 5 through 15. The Bahamian educational system is based on the traditional British model, in which students pass through various standards or levels:

Uniforms are the rule for schoolchildren in the Bahamas.

A school in Hope Town, Elbow Cay (population 450). Buildings are often painted white, with rich colors reserved for shutters and doors.

six years in primary school (ages 5–11), three years in junior high school (ages 11–14), two years in senior high school (ages 14–16), and two years in sixth form (ages 16–18). Students take periodic proficiency examinations: the Bahamas Junior Certificate at the end of junior high, the General Certificate of Education (GCE) "O" (Ordinary) levels at the end of senior high, and the GCE "A" (Advanced) levels at the end of sixth form. The first two examinations cover a wide range of subjects from English and math to science, arts, and physical education; one school in the Bahamas offers the sixth form course in science subjects leading to the GCE "A" levels.

There are several private adult vocational schools, as well as the College of the Bahamas (COB), established in 1974. The COB offers bachelor's degrees and two-year associate degrees, with credits that can be transferred to affiliated colleges in Britain, Canada, and the United States; a further two years' study at one of these colleges leads to a full degree. The Bahamas is affiliated with the University of the West Indies (UWI), which has campuses in Barbados, Jamaica, and Trinidad.

HEALTH AND WELFARE

The government-run Bahamian health care system covers the more populated islands. Nassau on New Providence has the largest public hospitals with state-of-the-art diagnostic equipment. Freeport on Grand Bahama has the government-run Rand Memorial Hospital. The other islands have clinics with resident doctors and nurses. Those who need specialist services not available in the Bahamas go to clinics in the United States, especially Florida, usually through a referral by their doctors. Many doctors who practice in the Bahamas are trained in medical colleges in the United States, Canada, Britain, or in the University of the West Indies.

A mandatory government-run insurance plan provides retirement, disability, medical, maternity, and funeral insurance. Premiums are deducted from workers' salaries, and employers also make contributions. The ratio of payments by worker and employer varies with the salary.

BUSH MEDICINE

Bahamians take advantage of the good medical care provided by public hospitals and clinics, but at the same time many of them, especially on the Family Islands, retain a strong belief in folk medicine to cure common ailments, and even some less common ones. Cerasee, a liquid concoction made from the plant *Mormodica charantia*, is said to be effective against anything from the common cold to cancer. The traditional Bahamian believes that a poultice of pepper leaves will reduce boils, dried goat droppings are effective against whooping cough, ground snails remove warts, and hog grease is a remedy for hair loss. Tea brewed from the leaves of a plant called five-finger or chicken-toe is believed to relieve body aches. A salve of white sage leaves is applied to the skin to soothe sufferers of chickenpox and measles. Wild guava is eaten by diabetics.

Of all the Family Islands, Cat Island is considered the stronghold of bush medicine, and many of the islanders there have the reputation of being effective healers. The island tradition in herbal remedies is included in the education program at the Rand Nature Center in Freeport, which displays exhibits and offers lectures on the subject.

*In Miami, perhaps
because many
Bahamians have
settled in southern
Florida, one sees
the Bahamian
influence in the
architecture of
some houses.
Bahamian Village
in Key West, an
island off the
Florida coast,
has an annual
celebration of
Bahamian
goombay music,
while in Miami,
a musical group
called the
Bahamas
Junkanoo Revue
creates Junkanoo
costumes for their
own parades and
even participates
in the Junkanoo
parades in
Nassau.*

THE IMPORTANCE OF MIAMI

The northern islands of the Bahamas lie close to the coast of Florida, the nearest being the Biminis, only 50 miles (80 km) away. Since the early 20th century, Americans have made the Biminis a vacation getaway, usually reaching the islands by yacht. The most famous of these is probably Ernest Hemingway, who described his experience in the Biminis in *Islands In The Stream.*

In recent years, the traffic has been in both directions. Making frequent trips across the narrow strip of the Atlantic dividing the two countries is the goal of many Bahamians. These can be for a short holiday, medical treatment at a hospital or clinic, or to visit friends, but the usual motive is to shop from the much wider selection of goods available on the American mainland. Clothes, electronic equipment, and housing materials are particularly in demand, and Bahamians can often be seen at the airport in Miami loaded down with such purchases. Import taxes in the Bahamas are extremely high and duty-free allowances comparatively low, so shopping is not a pastime that most Bahamians can indulge in nearly as often as they would like, but it explains why there are airplanes leaving every hour from Nassau airport to Miami.

DO'S AND DON'TS

Bahamians are an extremely hospitable and friendly people. Whether on a Family Island or in Nassau, New Providence, much of Bahamian life is lived outdoors, as the climate is quite dry and warm most of the year. It is common to see household members doing chores, just resting, or visiting with friends on the front porch. It is sociable to be outdoors, ready to greet neighbors and passers-by, and generally keep in touch with district affairs.

Showing respect to a casual acquaintance is an important custom. The correct greeting is always appreciated. For example, identifying oneself clearly is important to a Bahamian; a stranger who fails to do so will most likely be asked where he or she comes from. Ignoring someone who is making friendly overtures is considered the height of bad form. Returning hospitality is important and must be in kind, from a verbal or written expression of gratitude to taking someone out for a meal.

Personal questions are the norm. Bahamians are by nature curious people and they like to know all about people they meet. Yet they are seldom intrusive, for they also sense others' need for privacy. Their friendliness sometimes encourages people to make the mistake of being too open about other people, to gossip. Bahamians do this all the time with each other in fun, but jokes and gossip are shared only within their own circle.

Eye contact is quite rare. Bahamians also strongly discourage staring as they are at heart quite reserved and do not like being looked at aggressively. Confrontation of any sort does not go down well in the Bahamas, nor do frivolous or patronizing comments about individual people or their religious beliefs.

Above all, Bahamians are a relaxed and easygoing people with an engaging sense of humor and an elastic sense of time—they call it BT, or Bahamian Time. They always welcome people to their homes and to their islands, just as long as visitors understand the rules and do not overstep the bounds of island propriety or custom.

A Bahamian pauses in her work at a botanical garden in Nassau to welcome a visitor.

RELIGION

THERE ARE VERY FEW BAHAMIANS who are not Christian. This is mainly due to the overwhelming number of the population who are descended from either British migrants or from African slaves converted to Christianity by their original owners. There are a few Muslims and even fewer Hindus, migrants who came to the Bahamas for work-related reasons, but they are dwarfed by both the size and the fervor of the Christian community.

THE IMPORTANCE OF CHRISTIANITY

Christianity in its various forms is a very important part of the fabric of daily life in the Bahamas. For almost all Bahamians, going to church on Sunday is the rule, and many people keep a Bible handy in a drawer at home or at work to read in their spare moments. Religious celebrations, both national and personal, often see big religious processions and displays.

Where in the world but in the Bahamas could people once fly with an airline called "Trinity" or buy real estate from a company called "Put God First?"

Opposite: **The Columbus Landfall Park in San Salvador is marked by a stark white cross.**

Left: **A monastery in Nassau.**

Dressing well, complete with dress shoes and collared, long-sleeved shirts, is a Sunday ritual.

THE FAITHS OF THE BAHAMAS

Many denominations of the Christian faith can be found on the islands—Christian Bahamians may be Anglicans, Baptists, Church of God, Church of Jesus Christ of the Latter-day Saints, Church of Nazarene, Jehovah's Witnesses, Methodists, Seventh Day Adventists, Lutherans, or Roman Catholics. Churches run the gamut from almost cathedral-sized to small single-room buildings. No community worth its name would be without at least one church even if, as on the smaller islands, the minister may have to go island-hopping by mailboat to hold services.

The one thing that Bahamians of all denominations have in common, beside their obvious acceptance of the Christian faith, is that religion is a very serious matter to them and an integral part of their daily lives. Another characteristic is that many Bahamians like to participate unrestrainedly in the services of their chosen church. For instance, many Bahamian churches offer "testimony services" that give worshipers a chance to repent publicly of past sins and to seek forgiveness from the congregation as a whole.

SUPERSTITIONS

There is no apparent conflict between Bahamians' strict adherence to the Christian faith and their strong belief in supernatural spirits' ability to affect human lives. Such folk beliefs have been handed down through the generations and go back to the African ancestry of many black Bahamians. They are still practiced to some degree by even the most educated.

If a Bahamian thinks he has become the victim of some malicious spirit, he may mark a series of X's around himself and repeat the phrase "10, 10, the Bible, 10" to offset the bad influence. Someone who is really seriously concerned about an evil influence may also sprinkle a particular kind of grain called guinea grain around the place to keep malicious spirits so occupied (they have to pick up the grains one by one, counting them as they do so) they will not have time to do their evil work. Love potions are popular: "cuckoo soup" is a dark-colored broth believed to have tremendous powers; one sip and the victim is hooked, no matter what his or her feelings were toward the perpetrator, nor what the latter may look like.

Church is a place for worship indoors, and to socialize outdoors.

On the darker side, there are still Bahamians who believe in the black arts of Obeah—a kind of voodoo—which they think confers special powers on the believer. Although Obeah is officially banned in the Bahamas, it is still possible to find some people who practice it—Obeah practitioners are well-known in the community and even advertise under titles such as "spiritual healer" and "psychic advisor." Obeah practitioners believe in their ability to totally control the lives of other people under certain circumstances. Naturally shed parts of a person (hair, fingernails, etc.) or even dirty laundry are thought to be sufficient material for an Obeah practitioner to put a spell or curse on a victim. The only remedy is to find someone with stronger powers to remove it.

There is black and white Obeah magic. An example of white magic is a dream book: traditionalists keep one in the belief that good spirits will help them find prosperity, perhaps through winning a lottery.

LANGUAGE

THE OFFICIAL LANGUAGE of the Bahamas is English, and anyone who speaks a variant of it as their national tongue can communicate in the Bahamas, even if street Bahamian English sounds like no other language in the world. There are actually two different English language forms used in the Bahamas—"standard" Bahamian English and a Bahamian dialect with a structure that draws heavily on those of various African languages. It has the same musical rhythm one often hears among Caribbean islanders. "True true" Bahamians speak both types of English, crossing comfortably from one to the other. They know when to use the one more appropriate to a particular situation.

There are also some French Creole speakers among the Haitian immigrants, but this language is very much confined to their own community and very few "true true" Bahamians understand, much less speak, this special patois.

Opposite: **The signs lead in every direction, and from Nassau to Andros, English is spoken.**

Left: **All the lessons in school are in English, as the education system is based on the British model.**

When kidding around, workers are likely to break into dialect, but with a foreign customer, they use standard English.

TALKIN' BAHAMIAN

Standard Bahamian English follows the formal rules of British English—the "Queen's English" that is heard in Bahamian law courts, for example, or the English taught in schools. In those situations where standard English is appropriate, Bahamians speak with a distinctly British English accent, as opposed to an American one, for example. What makes the Bahamian spoken dialect in daily use unique is that it disregards many standard English rules. For example, the use of tenses often focuses entirely on the present regardless of the period of time concerned: "I gone to work yesterday" sums up the past, while "we see you tomorrow" takes care of the future. Similarly, plurals are created simply by the context ("I have four nice dress") and emphasis is provided through repetition ("that girl is pretty-pretty").

Bahamians also have some quite distinctive and unique words in their vocabulary, such as "boungy" (buttocks) or "grabalishus," which describes a greedy person. Some common English words show up in radically changed forms too. For instance it is quite possible in the Bahamas to catch "ammonia" (pneumonia) or even "browncurtis" (bronchitis).

Bahamian proverbs show a similar inventiveness of language. "It ain't for want of tongue that cow don't talk" means "Just because people have the ability to speak doesn't necessarily mean they always should." "The wind don't blow in the same dog tail all the time" means "Patience—your turn will come eventually."

All of this is spoken with a special lilt in the voice, often with a rising inflection at the end of a sentence and the addition of the word "eh" at the end if a question is being asked—"She be coming today, eh?"

PRONUNCIATION Standard English speakers may have to depend on context to follow a conversation in Bahamian patois because in fast-paced dialogue, words lose their consonants, have their vowels changed, or are otherwise rearranged by a transposition of letters. For example, "them" becomes *dem*, "woman" *ooman*, "man" *mon*, "film" *flim*, "you" *yo*, "thought" *tot*, and "smash" *'mash*. Endings are also lost, so that "cleaning" becomes *cleanin'*, "don't" *dun*, and "child" *chile*. Those accustomed to Jamaican patois will have little trouble, since the Bahamian version is more recognizable to the English speaker than Jamaican.

Two new experiences for these Japanese tourists—Bahamian talk and conch sashimi.

The American Loyalist Garden in Great Abaco is a monument to Loyalist ancestors. They are remembered also in their family names.

NAMES, BABY!

Bahamians have elevated the invention of first names to a fine art, possibly because there are surprisingly few surnames around in the Bahamas. Many surnames go back to the British Eleutherian Adventurers or the white Loyalist settlers of the 17th and 18th centuries, for example Albury, Higgs, Johnson, Smith, or Stubbs. Also, all the slaves belonging to one owner carried his surname.

The wide variety of unusual first names in modern Bahamas shows the creativity that goes into naming Bahamian children. This is done by choosing from a wide range of prefixes, combining these with a known name, and then sometimes adding a suffix as well, just for good measure. Other variables include adding the ethnic origin, or the name of a film star or royal personage. Royalty is a familiar theme, perhaps because the Bahamas was a favorite leisure spot with British royalty, among others.

Female first names include the uncomplicated Sarah or Jeanne and the far more exotic Lashandra, Rayniska, Raymondessa, or even Marilyn Monroe.

Male names could be anything from the biblical Abraham and John to Deshawn, Tameko, or even Prince Albert.

Satellite dishes give Bahamians a wide range of television programs.

KEEPIN' UP WIT' THE NEWS

Many Bahamians have a tendency to be preoccupied with gossip. Not surprisingly, therefore, considering the widespread nature of the country, continuous access to the media plays a most important part in keeping Bahamians happy and holding them together.

Radio Bahamas broadcasts throughout all the Bahamian islands nonstop via four stations, each offering different programming or focusing on a different geographic area. (On some islands, however, it is easier to tune in to Florida stations.) There is also a television service by the Bahamas Broadcasting Corporation, which offers programming for six hours daily on weekdays and 10 hours on weekends. In addition, most Bahamians have access to a wide range of programs from the United States using satellite dishes or subscribing to cable networks.

The *Nassau Guardian* and the *Tribune* are major newspapers published in Nassau and available in all the major islands. A daily newspaper, the *Bahama Journal*, is published in Freeport. But most Bahamians outside the major centers rely much more on broadcast news than they do on newspapers, for the news is old by the time newspapers arrive by mailboat at some of the more remote islands.

ARTS

BAHAMIANS EXCEL in the performing and visual arts, and they like nothing better than having an excuse to display their talents. Musicality seems to come naturally to the average Bahamian. This, combined with a flair for unique uses of color and decoration in folk art, and blended with both African and European traditions, leads to some unique expressions of Bahamian art.

MUSIC AND DANCE

Bahamians love to sing and dance and do both with tremendous enthusiasm. Songs are an intrinsic part of their oral tradition. Bahamian storytellers weave morals and myths into musical folktales. They call this musical improvisation ad-libbing, "rigging," or chatting, and use it not only for entertainment but also in church.

Opposite: **A musician plays steel drums in a hotel on Paradise Island.**

Left: **A rake'n'scrape band performs at a club in Freeport.**

The annual Junkanoo parades (described in the chapter on festivals) are by far the most popular form of expression in music and dance, but their popularity has much to do with goombay music, which is especially universal.

GOOMBAY In the islands the beat of goatskin drums accompanied by bongos, conch-shell horns, maracas, rattles, "click" sticks, flutes, bugles, whistles, and cowbells can be heard all year round in both impromptu and rehearsed performances. The different renditions of goombay are quite unique; the only common thread running through it all is a fast-paced, regular, and sustained melody.

Goombay music was imported a few centuries ago through the slave trade from the west coast of Africa. It is a mixture of rhythmic African drumming ("talking drums" were used in communication over distances) and traditional slave songs developed during the many years of black oppression on the North American continent.

Today, goombay music is commercially packaged in all the tourist hotels, where colorful, ruffle-sleeved dancers (usually male) gyrating to the goombay beat are the expected entertainment. As it is a part of the Junkanoo festival in December, people sometimes refer to it, incorrectly, as Junkanoo music. Every summer, beginning around June, the islands reverberate in a four-month-long goombay festival. A popular goombay artist in the United States is Tony Mackay, formerly of Cat Island but now living in Miami. He is something of a cult figure, known for his outrageous costumes and long, braided hair.

RAKE'N'SCRAPE Another kind of music found throughout the islands, usually played in bars and clubs and during festivals and regattas, is "rake'n'scrape." This is impromptu music played on accordions and guitars, usually accompanied by a variety of homemade instruments ranging from shakers made of seed-filled pods to saws played with household implements.

REGGAE, RAP, SOCA, CALYPSO, HIP-HOP, AND R&B are other rhythms that have emerged in the Bahamas in the past decade. They are often integrated with goombay sounds, but one usually has no problem identifying the different musical styles. Reggae and calypso are sounds associated with Jamaica, while soca is a Caribbean dance music with a pounding beat derived from calypso and American soul music.

SPIRITUALS and church music are close to the Bahamian soul. Attending church and participating in the choir is very important to Bahamians, so most churches have a well-developed choral music tradition. Spirituals brought to the Bahamas by slaves from North America feature predominantly here. There are many variants of these, including the call-and-answer type of singing in which the choir and the congregation exchange questions and answers in song—this is the chatting or "rigging" that is part of Bahamian music.

Opposite: **Gospel singers hum and clap a rhythm on Great Exuma island. They improvise the words and melody as they sing in praise of God.**

Above: **Two paintings in the Albert Lowe Museum in New Plymouth, where exhibits have Loyalist themes. Albert Lowe was a Loyalist shipbuilder, and several generations of Lowes lived in the Abacos.**

Opposite: **Woodcarvings on sale in Nassau.**

LITERATURE

Recently a growing number of books have been written by Bahamians about the Bahamas. Among the best of these are the thriller *Bahamas Crisis* by Desmond Bagley and several books written by Patricia Glinton-Meicholas on Bahamian life and culture, especially *How to be a True True Bahamian* and *Talkin' Bahamian*. Although only partly about the Bahamas, the actor Sidney Poitier's autobiography *This Life* offers insights into life on Cat Island where he was born and raised. Another Bahamian autobiography that the islanders enjoy reading is Captain Leonard Thompson's historical *I Wanted Wings*. Marion Bethel is a well-known Bahamian poet whose writing has appeared in American literary journals. She was awarded the Casa de las Americas Prize in 1994 for her book of poems, *Guanahani, My Love*.

VISUAL ARTS

Only recently has there been a flourishing of indigenous Bahamian painting. Many contemporary Bahamian artists use the Bahamas as their inspiration, painting landscapes and seascapes, Bahamian houses, Junkanoo dancers and musicians, and other Bahamians in brightly colored settings. Some Bahamian artists are a little offbeat, such as Janine Antoni who made headlines in 1993 when she lowered her naked body into a bathtub of animal fat! A leading Bahamian artist who has inspired young Bahamian artists is Amos Ferguson, whose primitive oils on cardboard carry four main themes: history, religion, nature, and folklore. Antonius Roberts is a Bahamian artist who is also an environmentalist. *The Last of the Casuarina*

Tree, an art installation he assembled for an exhibition, has casuarina tree trunk remnants and *kalik* bottles filled with sand, letters, and editorials written in support of the casuarina trees that the government planned to remove from coastal areas in Nassau. (Traditional Bahamians hang *kalik* bottles on tree branches as a protection against evil.)

HANDICRAFTS

Traditional handicrafts have always been a part of the Bahamian lifestyle. With increasing tourist arrivals crafts have become an important local industry. Particularly at the Nassau Straw Market, visitors can find a wide range of products that are shipped there from other Bahamian islands. The popular ones are manufactured from natural materials such as straw dried from wild grasses. Straw products include bags, hats, baskets, dolls, placemats, floor mats, and various household utility items. Most of these are entirely handmade, a simple sewing machine being the only mechanical equipment used.

Hardwood carvings and small pieces of furniture are also popular. The local artists also make ceramic pottery: tumblers and figurines are memorabilia for the tourists, some carrying famous signatures including Amos Ferguson's.

LEISURE

THE NEARLY PERFECT BAHAMIAN CLIMATE encourages people to spend much of their leisure time outdoors. With such easy access to the sea and lovely beaches close at hand, it is not surprising that many Bahamian leisure activities center around the sea, although there are lots of attractions on land as well.

SWIMMING AND BEACHES

One of the most interesting facts about the Bahamas is that, although there is no official racial segregation, through custom and usage many of the country's major beaches tend to be used by either black or white Bahamians—but not by both at the same time. In the more populated islands, such as New Providence and Grand Bahama, major hotels monopolize many of the best beaches, with the result that these are mostly used by white Bahamians and tourists.

Opposite and left: **The sea provides ideal recreation for Bahamians and tourists, from sunbathing around hotel pools while enjoying the sea air to speedboat racing. Others match their skills with like-minded people in a game of beach volleyball.**

The hotel beaches are beautifully maintained and many of them offer access to inshore coral reefs, enabling the more timid to enjoy the experience of snorkeling without having to venture too far into the water. Many black Bahamians go to the more secluded, less developed beaches. Simply sitting on the sand and *conversatin'* takes up as much of their time (or more) as actually being in the water.

BOATING AND SAILING

Bahamian residents seem to prefer spending their time on top of the water rather than in it, so "messing around" in boats of all shapes and sizes is quite popular. A sizeable number of Bahamians own boats and use them for a variety of purposes, often chartering them out to the tourists for island-touring or for deep-sea sport fishing.

DIVING AND SNORKELING

The islands are a diving and snorkeling paradise. Many local companies cater to people who want to learn or practice either activity. It is easy to see the attraction of scuba-diving for both locals and tourists as the sea around the islands is full of exotic marine life and numerous old wrecks whose nooks and crannies make

interesting places to explore. The water temperature remains constant the whole year round, which means it is possible to dive without a wet suit at any time. The underwater visibility is usually exceptionally good.

Experienced scuba-diving enthusiasts like to try wall or cave diving, although neither of these are for the more cautious as they often involve descents of more than 100 feet (30 m) in order to get into one of the underwater blue holes or caves. Snorkeling is a less dangerous pastime and requires only a mask, a breathing tube, and flippers. Swimming near the surface of one of the many Bahamian coral reefs, the snorkeler can see a colorful variety of fish and marine life, ranging from moray eels and turtles to angelfish and parrotfish. For those who want to join in and swim with some of the bigger fish but are not prepared to scuba-dive or snorkel on their own, a number of Bahamian companies offer experiences such as swimming with dolphins or even sharks.

Above: **A diver conceals herself to observe a school of grunts swim past.**

Opposite: **A catamaran sails toward the white beach of Paradise Island.**

SPRING BREAK IN THE BAHAMAS

College vacations see crowds of American students congregate at resorts in the Bahamas. Student group organizers set up stations, sometimes just a table and a few chairs outside their hotel, and dispense advice. They also keep a check on the behavior of members in their groups, for Bahamian authorities are on guard against undesirable behavior, especially in large groups of vacationing students. They like to maintain an image of the Bahamas as a desirable family resort destination.

There is no bad time to go, except that the southern islands may be uncomfortably warm in the summer, and one must be prepared for some wet weather in the winter. Loose-fitting cotton clothes, sandals, and protection from the sun—all easily packed into one carry-on bag—take care of personal effects for a week's fun by the sea, while those who prefer hiking need sturdier clothes and shoes for protection from thorny bushes and rocky limestone ground. Carousing does not end when the sun goes down, and student vacationers are generally well prepared for evenings of entertainment in some of the hotels that dot the beach fronts of the Bahamian islands.

FISHING

Fishing is popular with both Bahamians and tourists. There are many possibilities, ranging from the simple hook and line to working with all the complex gear of a deep-sea fishing expedition.

The bonefish is highly sought after in the Bahamas. These large-eyed, very bony fish can weigh from 5 to 10 pounds (2.3–4.5 kg) and be more than a foot long. They are challenging to catch as they never stay in one place long and are extremely sensitive to sound. Bigger fish that provide sport for Bahamian fishermen include wahoo (many local tournaments are dedicated to catching wahoo), snapper, grouper, and marlin. Sport fishing is quite tightly regulated in Bahamian waters. Permits are needed for deep-sea fishing, and there are limits on how much fish can be caught by a single angler. There is no lack of charter boats to take enthusiasts to deeper waters to fish for sport fish like the large blue marlin and tuna.

LAND SPORTS

The number of golf courses has increased dramatically over the last few years. It is now possible to play golf on most of the islands of the Bahamas, although New Providence and Grand Bahama have the most prominent courses. Clubs organize tournaments regularly and the Bahamas hosts leading international tournaments.

In spite of the British heritage of the Bahamas, cricket has become much less important in recent years than it used to be, and still is in many other former colonies. It used to be played fairly frequently, but since the 1970s it has given way to other, more American-oriented sports such as baseball, basketball, softball, and football.

Cricket season in Nassau.

HIKING, CYCLING, AND RIDING

The islands have coastal trails, and there are tracks running through many nature reserves, but the terrain inland is generally rough and overgrown with bushes. Hikers have to beware of sinkholes concealed beneath low bushes. Cycling and riding are less common on the islands, except at a few resorts that provide good roads for cyclists. Yet Grand Bahama hosts a 100-mile (160 km) road race for cycling enthusiasts every year, while an organization on Eleuthera organizes week-long cycling trips. Mountain bikes fare better on the rough Bahamian terrain.

BIRDWATCHING

The Bahamas is one of the world's best places to go birdwatching. There are numerous nature reserves dotted around the islands that are protected habitats for over 5,000 bird species, one of the most spectacular being the Bahamian national bird, the pink flamingo.

CASINOS AND GAMBLING

A recently popular activity in the Bahamas is gambling in one of the several casinos that have sprung up on the more populated islands. To prevent the local economy from being devastated instead of enhanced by the advent of casinos the government has enacted a law to prevent Bahamian residents from gambling in the casinos—gambling there is strictly for foreigners. Bahamians enter casinos for other entertainment or to work.

TRADITIONAL PASTIMES

Traditional games like *warri* are part of the African heritage of the majority of Bahamians. Dominoes, checkers, and many varieties of card games are also still popular. Storytelling is an important part of the Bahamian leisure tradition. The telling of tales of magic and supernatural heroes has died out, but tales based on family history and local events, especially tales of disaster, are commonplace and appreciated by both young and old.

A game of checkers at the quayside.

BAHAMIAN FESTIVALS are lavish, long-lasting, and loud. Most of them tie in with Christian festivals and some are expressions of national pride. But none exemplifies the Bahamian spirit better than the Christmas and New Year's festival no "true true" Bahamian would miss—Junkanoo.

JUNKANOO

No one knows for certain how this festival got its name, although some have suggested that it came from "Johnny Canoe," an African folk hero and a tribal chief who demanded the right to celebrate with his people even after being made a slave. Many other people think the name came from the French words *gens inconnu* (alien or unknown people). If this is true, it is appropriate for this festival because participants in a Junkanoo parade are masked to conceal their identity.

Bahamians spend months preparing their costumes for Junkanoo. Those who miss the spectacle can enjoy the creativity that goes into the costumes at any time since the best ones are displayed in a museum in Nassau.

Left: The Independence Day parade takes place on July 10. Two other national holidays are Emancipation Day (first Monday in August) and Discovery Day (October 12). The first celebrates the emancipation of the slave ancestors of the majority of Bahamians while the second commemorates Columbus's arrival at San Salvador.

Opposite: Prizes are given for the best Junkanoo costumes, motivating participants to create unique masks and hats out of colored crepe paper.

Participants dress up in a dazzling variety of colorful costumes, known as "scrap," complete with hats and masks representing mythical and imaginary characters. They parade down the length of Bay Street in Nassau (the biggest Junkanoo parade in the Bahamas) and the main streets of other smaller towns to the accompaniment of goombay music made with goatskin drums, gourds, cowbells, conches, horns, and whistles. The crowds lining the streets join in with or without instruments, imitating the "ka-lik, ka–lik" sound of the cowbells. The object is to be as flamboyant and to make as much noise as possible.

Preparations for Junkanoo begin up to a year before the first "rush," as the parade is known, and are often very elaborate. Most of the participants belong to one of the many competing groups sanctioned by the national Junkanoo committee, which awards prizes for the best costumes and music. These groups—which can sometimes number up to 500 members and which give themselves names such as Saxons, Pigs, Valley Boys, or Music Makers—usually decide well in advance on a theme that will be reflected in the costumes of their members. The exact details of what everyone will be wearing and what they will represent are closely guarded secrets until they assemble for the parade.

Other individuals can also take part in the Junkanoo procession—and their costumes are every bit as fanciful as the group ones—though not usually as elaborate. There are minimum requirements for costumes in a Junkanoo parade, but usually the more colorful and fantastic the better.

Sartorial splendor in a many-colored cape and a hat decorated with crepe paper.

Participants of Junkanoo parades express their creativity in unique ways.

Cardboard and crepe paper are common construction materials for the Junkanoo costumes, and paint and "tricks"—beads, satin, plastic jewels among them—are used to embellish them. Because of the fragile nature of such materials, however, and the exuberance with which their wearers move about during the parade itself, many costumes do not survive the parade in very good condition. Fortunately the best of them have been preserved by collectors and many are on display in the Junkanoo museum, a new feature of the Nassau waterfront.

The parade begins at 3 or 4 a.m. on Boxing Day, the day after Christmas, with streetlights shining on a sea of strange and wonderful characters. During the parade, they stop and perform their dances at designated places along the route, while the drummers show off their amazing skill. This is called a "breakout." When the parade continues, spectators join in, dancing to the music behind the performers. When the dancing ends, people gather for the prize-giving, after which the celebration draws to a close at about dawn. People straggle home exhausted, to recoup their energy for the second "rush," on New Year's Day.

Goombay dancers are usually male, but hotel shows featuring goombay music often employ dancers of both genders.

"Goombay" is said to be derived from the African word nkumbi. In the Bantu language, it describes a type of ceremonial drum.

THE GOOMBAY SUMMER FESTIVAL

There are many reflections of the Junkanoo experience at other times of year besides December—one of the tourist hotels even sponsors a mini Junkanoo procession every Friday night. Nothing comes close to the actual Christmas celebration, but one of the best replicas is the summer goombay festival that combines the exuberance of a Junkanoo procession with goombay music performances.

REGATTAS AND OTHER MAJOR EVENTS

Whatever the time of year, some major party is happening in one of the islands. Chances are this will be a regatta, where the main show is a boat race, while sideshows such as beauty pageants and cooking demonstrations are enjoyed by noncompetitors. It may be a pineapple festival, a conch-cracking contest, or a historical weekend to celebrate Loyalist roots. In all of these, music and food are always prominently featured.

NATIONAL HOLIDAYS

Among the public holidays Bahamian Independence Day and Emancipation Day. Independence Day is on July 10, but the celebration lasts a week, with speeches, parades, and fireworks. Emancipation Day, observed on the first Monday in August, celebrates the anniversary of the freeing of slaves throughout the British colonies. In Nassau, the end of slavery is also celebrated in a more local way during Fox Hill Day, which takes place on the second Tuesday in August. Fox Hill Day owes its origin to the fact that it took about 10 days for news of freedom from slavery to reach the then somewhat isolated community of Fox Hill. Another Bahamian holiday is Discovery Day, October 12, which commemorates the landing of Christopher Columbus on the island of San Salvador in 1492.

Easter is celebrated in Nassau with parties and Easter egg hunts. The holiday includes Good Friday, Easter Monday, and Whit Monday seven weeks after Easter.

On November 5, bonfires are seen everywhere in celebration of Guy Fawkes Day, a British import that has nothing to do with the Bahamas, but the fun-loving Bahamians think it a good excuse to party! So the instigator of the 1605 Gunpowder Plot to blow up the British Houses of Parliament is burnt in effigy, and his death is further commemorated by extravagant displays of fireworks.

Public holidays are also occasions for extended Bahamian families to gather for a special homecoming celebration, with feasts, parties, songs, and long sessions of storytelling.

A Bahamian is never too old to enjoy some Easter goodies.

FOOD

MANY DAILY ACTIVITIES in the Bahamas are conducted either around the dining table or with a plate of one of the local delicacies close at hand. The contents of a meal and the sophistication of the dishes can differ from island to island, but the portions are always substantial. Due to the influence of the many different races of people who have lived in the Bahamas over the last 500 years, the cuisine is quite varied.

The long-gone Lucayans' diet was predominantly seafood. This was supplemented with cassava, corn, and sweet potatoes, all of which are native to the Bahamas. British meat pies and roasts followed in their wake, but North American cuisine has taken over in popularity. The African influence is present in grits, johnnycakes, and peas'n'rice, as well as in the flavorings. Bahamian flavoring ingredients include salt, nutmeg, ginger, chili peppers, lime, parsley, thyme, and tarragon.

Opposite: **A delicious conch chowder served in a Bahamian restaurant.**

Left: **Fruit of the Bahamas—bananas, sugar apples, and coconut.**

CONCH

Although seafood in general plays a big part in the modern Bahamian diet, none is more common or more universally enjoyed than the conch. Conch (pronounced "konk") is a snail-like mollusk found all over the Bahamas, and its white, pink-fringed meat forms the basis of many dishes. It can be fried, grilled, steamed, stewed, or made into a raw conch salad, the conch meat diced and mixed with chopped onion, tomato, cucumber, and celery, then liberally sprinkled with pepper and lime juice.

After a first taste, a newcomer might wonder why a not particularly appetizing meat is eaten so often by Bahamians—from gourmet dishes in fancy restaurants to conch fritters called "cracked" conch in small stalls on sidewalks. There are two reasons—conch is cheap and, more importantly, Bahamians believe it to be a potent aphrodisiac.

In Bahamas a conch cracking contest is held on Discovery Day. Conch cracking requires dexterity in removing the meat: first by hitting the shell with a heavy implement to break it (it must be hit in the right spot, where the meat is attached to the shell), then "jewking" the conch out of its shell by grasping an appendage (commonly called a foot or claw) and pulling it.

OTHER SEAFOOD

Crawfish (the Bahamian version of lobster) is also very popular, as is the land crab, which can be seen running around on many of the islands and is easily caught. It is often served stuffed with other food. From among the large variety of fish caught off the Bahamian coasts, grouper, a mild-flavored white fish, is a particular favorite. This is often served with a spicy Creole-style sauce, followed closely by baked bonefish with a hot pepper sauce. Outside the more populated centers, many other varieties of seafood find their way to the table—turtle dishes are popular on the Exumas, for instance, while other seafood recipes can feature such marine life as yellowtail, snapper, grunts, jacks, and even "goggle eyes."

Opposite: **Conch meat is rather slimy. Before it is eaten, the meat must be washed in a mixture of lime juice, salt, and water to remove the slime.**

Below: **Fillet of crawfish served in a gourmet restaurant.**

Rice cooked with pigeon peas and peppers, called peas'n'rice, with a generous portion of papaya for dessert.

One of the most common ways of preparing fish, especially for breakfast, is "boil fish" or "stew fish," a kind of fish stew in which a firm-fleshed fish (often grouper) is put in the pot with salt pork, onions, potatoes, celery, tomatoes, and seasonings and then boiled until the appetizing aroma is sufficiently strong to tempt the cook to tuck into sizeable helpings of the end result.

GRITS, PEAS, AND JOHNNYCAKE

Seafood and other meats are often eaten with side dishes, including some of the most traditional of all Afro-Bahamian foods—grits, peas'n'rice, and johnnycake. All three are quite similar in appearance to dishes eaten in the southern United States, and indeed many of these recipes came over from the American South with the slave ancestors of today's Bahamians.

A generous mound of grits, ground cornmeal mush, with vegetables added, often forms the basis of a meal. There are as many recipes for peas'n'rice as there are people, for it depends on the individual blending of ingredients, the cooking time, and the sauces poured over them. Ingredients can range from simply pigeon peas (*not* green peas) and rice to pigeon peas and rice with salt pork, tomatoes, thyme, green pepper, celery, or virtually any other ingredients an inspired cook might choose to add. As for seasonings, individual taste dictates what these should be, common ones being salt, whole peppercorns, allspice, chili peppers, and chopped onions.

Johnnycake, once considered poor man's food because it was the staple diet of impoverished early settlers, is a pan-baked bread made with milk, butter, flour, sugar, salt, and baking powder. Sometimes it is even baked in a sand-filled box on fishing boats. Johnnycake is rather bland to the taste, but it certainly fills the stomach.

Cookouts are a favorite Bahamian social gathering. A typical serving of barbecued meat usually comes with potato salad, conch salad or fritters, coleslaw, and macaroni.

SOUSE

A popular dish in the Bahamas, especially on the weekend, is souse. Very simple to prepare, it is popular because of its ability to fill an empty stomach, while at the same time it is very little work for the cook. The meat ingredients can be anything, from parts of a sheep, including the tongue, or parts of a pig, including the trotters, or chicken, or conch. These are tossed into a large pot of salted water and boiled with spices and other ingredients. When the meat is tender enough to eat, it is ladled onto plates, liberally sprinkled with lime juice and pepper, and eaten with bread.

There are different kinds of souse. In England, the meat parts (trotters and ears, for instance) are pickled in vinegar. In the Bahamas, however, spices are used in the cooking, and lime juice is added when serving, to give it a sour flavor.

GUAVA DUFF

Dessert is as substantial as the main course, and none more so than the absolute favorite, guava duff. A duff is a boiled pudding filled with fruit (usually guava, but it could be melon, pineapple, papaya, or mango), which has a cake-like consistency and is eaten with a sauce. Good Bahamian cooks have their own recipe, often handed down the generations and jealously guarded. A good guava duff is time-consuming to make.

GUAVA DUFF

Guava Jam:
12–15 guavas
1 tablespoon sugar, or to taste

Butter Sauce:
2 egg whites
1 cup butter
1 cup granulated sugar
2 teaspoons vanilla

Dough:
$^1/_4$ cup butter
$^1/_4$ cup shortening
$^1/_4$ cup sugar
2 egg yolks
3 cups flour
4 teaspoons baking powder
$^1/_2$ teaspoon salt
2 teaspoons vanilla

Prepare guava jam. Peel guavas and grate coarsely. Add sugar to taste.

Prepare butter sauce. Beat egg whites until foamy. Cream butter with sugar until light. Add egg whites and vanilla and continue beating until smooth. Set aside the sauce.

Prepare the dough. Beat butter, shortening, and sugar until smooth, then beat in egg yolks. Sift flour with baking powder and salt, and work it into the batter. Add vanilla. Divide the dough into 3 portions, shaping each into a ball. Refrigerate for 30 minutes.

Roll out each portion of dough into a rectangle, and spread with guava jam. Starting from one end, fold into a roll. Cover with aluminum foil, place in a baking bag, and seal. Boil in a large pot of water for 1 hour. Remove from water. Slice and serve warm with butter sauce.

PEAS'N'RICE

12 ounce (350 g) can of pigeon peas
1 onion, peeled and chopped
black pepper, thyme, and salt to taste

6 ounce (170 g) can tomato paste
6 cups water
6 cups rice

Sauté pigeon peas and chopped onion with the spices. Add tomato paste and stir until the ingredients are covered with the paste.

Add water and bring to a boil. Reduce the heat and cook until the sauce has reduced by half. Add rice and stir well.

Reduce the heat and cook until the liquid has been totally absorbed by the rice.

Serve topped with tomato sauce.

BAHAMIAN TOMATO SAUCE

1 tablespoon oil
1 onion, sliced
1 green pepper, chopped
1 stalk celery, chopped

1 tomato, chopped
black pepper, thyme and salt to taste
6 ounce (170 g) can tomato paste
1 cup water

Heat the oil. Sauté onion, green pepper, celery, tomato, and spices in oil until the onion slices are translucent. Add tomato paste and water and cook for another 2–3 minutes.

JOHNNYCAKE

1 cup all-purpose flour
1 cup cornmeal
1 teaspoon baking soda
$^1/_2$ teaspoon salt

1 tablespoon sugar
1 egg, beaten
1 cup buttermilk
3 tablespoons vegetable oil

Preheat oven to 400° Fahrenheit (250° Centigrade). Grease an 8 inch (20 cm) square pan with vegetable oil.

Sift together all the dry ingredients. Combine the egg and buttermilk and add all at once to the dry ingredients. Add oil. Stir (do not beat) until dry ingredients are just moistened. Put into the prepared pan and bake 25–30 minutes. Cut into 2 inch (5 cm) squares and serve.

Fresh produce is always available in market bazaars in Nassau.

One Bahamian fruit has a name that many people know although they may never have eaten the fruit. The jujube looks like a large, brown grape and has a crisp, pale yellow flesh surrounding a single pit. Its juice flavors the chewy candy known as jujubes.

TROPICAL FRUIT

Many varieties of locally grown fruit are eaten raw or form the basis of desserts and drinks. Some of these, such as bananas, papayas, pineapples, and mangoes, are well-known to Bahamians and others alike. Others, including soursops, sugar apples, sapodillas, and jujubes have flavors that may take a little time to appreciate.

The dark green, irregularly shaped soursop is covered with soft spines and weighs from 1 to 5 pounds (0.5–2 kg). Its fibrous, white pulp is refreshing; far from being sour, it is usually sweet with only a slightly tart flavor. The sugar apple belongs to the same family as the soursop (*Annona*). It looks like a green (sometimes purplish brown) pine cone about the size of a tennis ball. To eat it, one splits the soft fruit open by hand and spoons out its sweet, smooth, segmented white flesh, separating it from the shiny black seeds. The sapodilla is an oval, brown fruit about 2–3 inches (5–8 cm) across, with 3–6 black seeds. The flesh, which is pale brown and smooth but sometimes slightly grainy, has been likened to pear flavored with brown sugar.

DRINKS

Drinks in the Bahamas tend to fall into two categories—those concocted for and served mainly to the tourists who frequent casino resorts, and those that are consumed by the locals. All of the first category are based on different varieties of rum and include such exotic concoctions as the "Bahama Mama" (rum, bitters, creme de cassis, grenadine, nutmeg, and citrus juices), the "Goombay Smash" (coconut rum, Bacardi rum, and a mixed fruit punch), and the Yellow Bird (rum, creme de banana liqueur, Galliano, and apricot brandy mixed with orange and pineapple juice). Drunk in quantity, the cumulative effect of these deceptively smooth-tasting concoctions can soon be quite lethal!

Nassau Royale is a locally produced liqueur that is included in some of the more exotic concoctions, but drunk by itself, it has a very pleasant rum-based taste. Some Bahamians prefer to stick to less exotic fare. They drink their rum straight or with water, and find Kalik, the locally produced lager-style beer, very refreshing on a hot day.

For those who want nonalcoholic drinks, Bahamians prefer those that are typically refreshing in hot climates—fresh lime coolers, for instance, and the more traditional sodas such as Coke or Pepsi and ginger ale. Different fruit juices are quite popular also, as is bottled water, since the tap water is a little salty. Coffee and tea are popular too, but perhaps due to the British heritage of the Bahamas, tea is often much better prepared than coffee tends to be.

Rum cocktails are popular tourist drinks in Bahamian resorts.

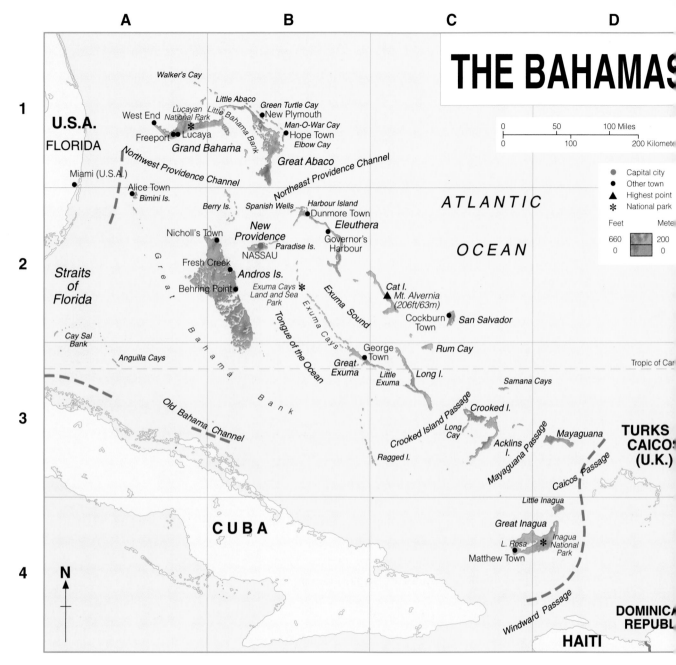

THE BAHAMAS

Walker's Cay

Little Abaco
Green Turtle Cay
New Plymouth
Man-O-War Cay
West End
Lucayan National Park
Little Bahama Bank
Freeport
Lucaya
Hope Town
Grand Bahama
Elbow Cay
Great Abaco

U.S.A.
FLORIDA

Northwest Providence Channel
Northeast Providence Channel

Miami (U.S.A.)

Alice Town
Bimini Is.

Berry Is.
Spanish Wells
Harbour Island
Dunmore Town
Eleuthera

ATLANTIC

OCEAN

Nicholl's Town
New Providence
Paradise Is.
NASSAU
Governor's Harbour

Fresh Creek
Andros Is.

Straits of Florida

Behring Point
Exuma Cays Land and Sea Park

Cat I.
Mt. Alvernia (206ft/63m)

Cockburn Town
San Salvador

Great Bahama Bank

Exuma Cays

Exuma Sound

Tongue of the Ocean

Cay Sal Bank

Anguilla Cays

George Town
Great Exuma
Little Exuma
Long I.

Rum Cay

Tropic of Cancer

Old Bahama Channel

Samana Cays

Crooked I.

Long Cay

Crooked Island Passage

Acklins I.

Mayaguana

TURKS CAICOS (U.K.)

Ragged I.

Mayaguana Passage

Caicos Passage

CUBA

Little Inagua

Great Inagua
L. Rosa
Matthew Town
Inagua National Park

N

Windward Passage

DOMINICA REPUBL

HAITI

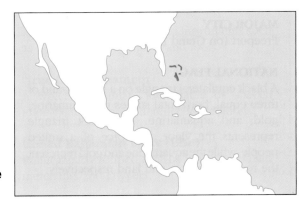

BIBLIOGRAPHY

Baker, Christopher P. *Lonely Planet Bahamas, Turks & Caicos*. Melbourne, Victoria, Australia: Lonely Planet Publications, 1998.

Fodor's 99 The Bahamas. New York: Fodors Travel Publications, 1998.

Frommer, Arthur and Darwin Porter. *Frommer's 2000 Bahamas*. Foster City, California: IDG Books Worldwide, 1999.

Hintz, Martin and Stephen V. *The Bahamas (Enchantment of the World)*. Danbury, Connecticut: Children's Press, 1997.

McCulla, Patricia E. *Bahamas (Major World Nations Series)*. Broomall, Pennsylvania: Chelsea House, 1998.

Whittier, Sara (editor). *Insight Guides: Bahamas*. New York: Langenscheidt Publishers, APA Publications, 1998.

INDEX

PICTURE CREDITS